Sell You
BEFORE
You Sell

boost your brand, close more sales,
and win your game.

Alex Rodríguez

Sell You Before You Sell

Boost your brand, close more sales, and win your game.

First Edition

Published 2018

YMMY Marketing, LLC (ymmymarketing.com)

ISBN 978-0-9906424-4-2

Written by Alex Rodríguez

Illustrations by Alex Rodríguez

Edited by Jessica Beeson

Cover design, diagrams, and layout by YMMY

Dedications

To Christ my Lord, who closed the most amazing sale in history, and to top it all, paid the price all by Himself.

To my dear Mami who poured her sacrificial love on me, and set the standard so high I can only wish to one day follow her example. You are amazing.

To Chava my love. You've been always by my side, and I will always be by yours. What else can I say? Te amo.

To the two arrows in my quiver, Nathan and Seth. Go forth and pierce through mediocrity in everything you do. Shoot high and never, ever low.

To anyone who has told me that my words or my life has pushed you forward in any meaningful way. In my moments of darkness, you shed light to help me keep focus on my purpose.

Table Of Contents

Introduction

What is the value of being the first person to pop up in someone's mind, right when they need a particular service performed?

How valuable would it be to increase the success rate of your sales appointments to such a degree that you can double or triple your business?

What if you could increase your authority so that people that meet with you are less resistant, and your sales go through more smoothly?

This is exactly what I intend to show you in this book. You will learn what I have personally done to raise my closing rates, wipe away objections before they even come up, and ultimately grow my business.

Although I'll be talking about sales, this isn't a book on sales training. You won't find techniques around which words to say to close harder, the five steps of a successful sales presentation, none of that. In fact, you'll barely find anything here about what to do during your sales appointments. Although I could share ideas and insights on what has worked for me during my sales appointments, that's not really the point of this book.

I would be dishonest if I told you that the only thing you need to close more sales is to employ an arsenal of trick phrases and scripts at your next sales appointment. If you're only thinking about your performance during the sales appointment, you are missing out on what really makes a difference.

This book is about the art and science of selling before you even set up the sales appointment. It's about selling before you even get into contact with someone for the first time.

In the next chapter, I'll explain why that word "selling" is in italics. Here I'll ask you an important question: Do you believe that "selling" is a bad word?

I know many people who do believe that selling is a topic they should avoid at all costs. They would say things like "I'm just not a salesperson,"

or "I'm just terrible at sales," or "Salespeople are just too pushy." If you asked me this same question four or five years ago, I would have said the same thing! It wasn't until a friend pat me on the back and gave me these wise words of advice that I began to understand the concept of selling. This friend turned to me one day and said, "If you're in business, then you're in sales."

Having learned my lesson, I'll go even farther and say: You are always selling.

One of the dictionary's definitions of the verb "to sell" goes like this: "To give up a property to another for something of value."

In a broad sense, if you are in business, you are always presenting people with something valuable in exchange for something that they own.

Yet as mentioned before, for some strange reason, the concept of selling fell into the swamp of undesirable concepts, along with liars, crooked politicians, people who text and drive, friends who spoil TV shows on social media, and other things we just hate. Maybe it was the door-to-door vacuum cleaner salesman's fault, I don't know. What I do know is that so many people resist the idea of selling, even though they are selling every single day of their lives.

Yes, I mean it. You are selling 24/7, 365 days of the year, all the time.

You may not realize it, and you may even want to fight against this fact. I would have been the first one to resist this idea, if it weren't because I discovered the effect it has had on my ability to grow in business. And it all begins with accepting the fact that we are always selling.

Now, if it's true that you are always selling, then it's also true that more of that "always" time is spent before and after your sales appointments than during them. Let me explain this another way: Let's imagine that one of your sales appointments lasts one hour. As far as that single sales encounter, you were selling in person for that single hour, but were also selling for hundreds of hours before the appointment. If we consider one month of your time, that single in-person sales appointment was 0.13% of your actual time selling.

Yes, you are selling way before you present others with the opportunity of a business transaction.

Let's face it, in this era of fast-moving communication, offering your services so they can contract you does not impress anyone. Buyers now come to sales meetings more equipped than ever, with more information and insights than at any other moment in history.

These decision-makers are either sold on your solution before the first minute of the first sales appointment begins, or might be convinced that they will not purchase that day. The most influential factor that will affect the sales outcome will be how well you have sold yourself before this moment.

People only invest in what they know and trust, never what someone merely presents them. If they aren't deeply convinced that what you offer is the right fit for them, they will never buy from you.

To convince them, you need to build that knowledge and trust, which happens most powerfully before the sales appointment.

Here's an example that happened to me fairly recently. This kind of situation actually happens to me all the time, but I have one stunning experience in mind as I write this.

I once met a guy at a networking meeting. Shake of hands, a few words exchanged, here's my business card, thanks for yours, and that's it. We really didn't spend a long period of time talking.

A month or so later, he reaches out to me via email, telling me that he had a problem with his business, and as he thought about different ways to solve it, my name came to mind. He then asked me for an appointment where I could present what I could do for his company.

Now keep in mind, before he reached out, I had not sent him a brochure, nor asked him to meet for coffee, none of that…yet without doing any of these "sales tactics", I came to his mind, and he requested an appointment from me. His brain did the work of automatically connecting his business' need with my name.

Please don't misunderstand me. There is absolutely nothing wrong with sending a brochure or asking to get together with someone to find out more about them and their needs. I'm just saying that in this situation, I didn't do any of these things, and yet, I was the first person he thought of as someone who could solve his company's need.

Ultimately, I did end up arranging a sales meeting and I did close a five-figure deal with this company without much back and forth or hesitation on their part. The process went as smoothly as it could have.

Pretty cool, right? Well, I won't tell you here what I did — or what I continue to do on a consistent basis — to make this happen. Do you know why I won't tell you?

Because that's what the rest of this book is for.

CHAPTER 1

Two Types of Sales

To Sell Or To Sell?

In the previous pages, I used the word "sell" with different meanings. The first meaning we'll dig into in this chapter doesn't need explaining, as it's the meaning you're most likely familiar with. I'm talking about passing goods from one hand to another with a delivery of currency in return. It's what we normally call *a transaction*.

If you're in a consultative practice, you sell when a potential client examines your deliverables and outcomes, and decides to pay you for your assistance. Depending on the stage you're in, you may call it "presenting a proposal," "hiring," "signing the contract," "getting the deal," or some other term. In the end, it comes down to good ol' *selling*.

It's safe to say that you'll never approach a random person on the street and offer your services, nor would you expect someone to come to you out of the blue and hire you while you were just sipping on a latte macchiato at your local coffee shop.

Selling directly — meaning, presenting value to a person without prior experience with you, your product, or your company — is perfectly fine for lower-ticket items. If all someone needs to purchase is a couple of tomatoes at the grocery store, a bottle of aspirin, or a can of tennis balls, you don't really need to spend efforts on presenting your authority ahead of time. If my son has a lemonade stand on a fairly populated corner on a sunny Saturday morning, he'll probably sell quite a few glasses of lemonade — at the very least, because of the amazingly charming way he can say "Sir, would you like some delicious lemonade?"

In the case of most high-ticket services, a prior relationship with a *brand* is absolutely essential. Why? Because a transaction of this sort requires a bit more consideration on the buyer's part. People usually have questions that need to be answered before they make a serious decision to invest in your services.

Research shows that in business to business sales, 86% of businesses open a project with a clear preference for one particular supplier, even though they might interview more than one. In other words, 8 out of every 10 business opportunities already seem to have the winner pre-selected *before* they place a request for proposals.[1] This is also true in consumer sales. According to Nielsen,[2] 92% of consumers say that they trust recommendations from people they know, while only around one third of them said they trusted traditional advertising.

> "It seems like those who establish their authority and credibility — their brand — most successfully, wins before the game even begins."

It seems like those who establish their authority and credibility — their *brand* — most successfully, wins before the game even begins.

There are many great definitions for the word "brand," but I'd like to use an extremely simple one here. A *brand* is a clear expectation towards a particular experience.

It's much more likely that someone will pay higher amounts for brands they have a clear expectation toward, because they can more easily

1 *"What is the B2B buying process?"* by Andrew Dalglish, www.circle-research.com/2017/map-of-the-b2b-buying-process/)

2 *"Consumer Trust In Online, Social And Mobile Advertising Grows"* by Nielsen Resarch, nielsen.com/us/en/insights/news/2012/consumer-trust-in-online-social-and-mobile-advertising-grows.html

visualize the experience they'll receive after making the transaction. This expectation can come from many sources. For example, a previous purchase of the same brand, a recommendation from someone else, or some kind of valuable information they consumed can leave a customer with a high expectation of that service. After any of these, they will come to the sale with a clear picture of what they're getting for their money.

Yet it's practically impossible to cause someone to have an expectation if they aren't first paying attention. In other words, if someone has no reason to pay attention to you, you will never have the opportunity to generate a picture in their mind of what to expect when they do business with you. On top of this, inviting others to pay attention to you is becoming more difficult with every year that passes.

Today we live in a hectic, information-saturated world. We've coined terms like FOMO — Fear Of Missing Out — to refer to our incessant need to be mentally plugged into information sources and consuming the latest and greatest updates, whether they are signals or just noises. Our attention span is now smaller than that of a goldfish.[3] It's becoming more and more difficult to catch people's attention in the middle of the distractions that tickle their brains on a consistent basis.

And yet, unless they decide to pay attention to us, we will never get a chance to create the expectation needed to have an opportunity to sell to them.

"Pay attention!" Have you ever noticed how we normally use those words? We refer to attention as something we *pay* to others. Yet, I don't think we treat this payment as what it is, an actual *transaction*.

This is the other type of selling I want to talk about: The Transaction of *Attention*.

---

3 Source: Harald Weinreich, Hartmut Obendorf, Eelco Herder, and Matthias Mayer: *"Not Quite the Average: An Empirical Study of Web Use,"* in the ACM Transactions on the Web, vol. 2, no. 1 (February 2008), article #5.

We *pay attention* to things that are valuable, while at the same time, we refuse to pay for anything that won't add to our experience. If it doesn't satisfy a need, desire, or aspiration, we move on towards the next diversion in our lives, whether it be binging on that new show, a mobile game we just downloaded and can't stop playing (that one we knew we shouldn't have downloaded, but we did anyway), or just the incessant chatter inside our own heads.

> "Attention is the most valuable currency of our day. If someone thinks about your brand for more than four seconds, you win."

At any given time, people have a certain amount of attention available from their daily "attention wallet," and whatever idea they find worthwhile or attractive gets a payment of that attention. Today, there are more things than ever competing for these types of transactions. There are so many players in the business of getting people to pay attention to them, and it's a rough contest. Attention is the most valuable currency of our day. If someone thinks about your brand for more than four seconds, you win.

Some might think that I'm going too far by calling attention a currency, but from where I see things, attention has most of the characteristics of a currency system. It's in limited supply. It's generally acceptable and desirable. It's portable. It's indestructible, and it's valid payment for something valuable.

In fact, a group of founders and developers have developed a cryptocurrency based on the idea of giving actual market value to our daily human attention. They're creating a system in which you can pay and exchange with your attention just as you would with any other government-issued currency system. This initiative may or may not succeed, but the fact is that many are waking up to the fact that our attention is an extremely valuable currency at our disposal.

Therefore, it's reasonable to think of the act of persuading others on *why* they should pay attention to your message as a type of selling. If we happen to be successful with the *transaction of attention*, then in exchange, we get a moment of their focus and their thoughts. Let me repeat this: We gain a person's **most valuable currency** when we present them with a reason *why* they should focus on a valuable idea we present them.

When they pay us their attention, something amazing happens. At that point, we get an open door to generate an expectation in their mind and in their heart. Ultimately, when they have this expectation, we've set the perfect environment to present our services in exchange for money.

Here is another look at the process:

Attention (1st Transaction) ›-› Expectation ›-› Sale (2nd Transaction)

The reason people find it so difficult to close more sales of the second kind is that they haven't closed enough sales of the first kind. They just haven't had enough successful transactions of attention with anyone. As a result, there is very little expectation surrounding their brand, and very few people place value on the service they offer.

This is often typical in highly commoditized industries, where each professional is not much different than the next one. You might have even felt the pain of a perfectly qualified prospect passing you by, or even choosing another competing consultant over you.

"The reason people find it so difficult to close more sales of the second kind is that they haven't closed enough sales of the first kind."

In the deepest part of your being, you *know* you're absolutely different than everyone else in your field. The problem is... *people you could do business with* don't know it.

And the reason they don't know what makes you different is that by default, they don't really *expect* you to be any different from anyone else.

They don't expect you to be different because — you guessed it — they've never been sold on *paying attention* to those aspects that make you so different from everyone else in your field. Would you blame them? In reality, they haven't paid any attention to you because nobody has ever persuaded them why they should.

But if you can sell *why* they should pay attention to you, you'll be able to sell almost anything afterwards.

CHAPTER 2

The Three Gaps

The Three Gaps

With new developments in technology and communication almost every single day, when you read that "times have changed," your instinctive response is almost always, "Well, DUH! Of course things change." We're used to feeling that we are always behind the trend. There's always some technique, device, technology... always something that is ahead of where we are, which we have not yet begun to implement into our daily lives.

I feel left behind all the time. Just the other day, my sister mentioned three or four productivity techniques that she follows on a consistent basis which I hadn't even heard about. I'm sure that if I study up and implement those, there will be four more new ones that make these ones irrelevant and make me feel like a Slugosaurus Rex. It's just normal to slip behind what actually works in the time we live in.

If you take a quick glance at how consultative professionals perform sales today, you will notice that there are a few things people are doing in clear contrast to what actually works today, creating a real disconnect between the way they show up and what decision-makers are really looking for.

The result of this disconnect is that a sales appointment is set with three huge gaps of understanding between them, which results in either:

a) The consultative professional is forced to climb a steep peak to try to close the sale, causing him/her to drop their value, increase the number of deliverables, or walk away without the sale.

b) The hiring party drops their expectation of value, which causes them to be disappointed before they get to experience the solution. This causes them to either begin the working relationship on the wrong foot, or are left with very little incentive to move forward and hire them.

When you approach a sales meeting without addressing these gaps, you are only doing a disservice to your own professional practice. You are wasting opportunities, time, and resources, which would be better spent preparing for this moment.

Let's talk about the three gaps that stand in your way when showing up and presenting your value.

GAP #1: EXPECTATION OF VALUE

In any field, it used to be fine to demand that value be provided after the monetary transaction was completed. First, you pay. Then you get your goods. This may be the way you currently handle your business, and it's the way millions of others still do it.

But that's not the way people hire services today.

Most people expect value to be provided before the sales process even begins, way before money exchanges hands. Once they have received value, then they open up to the consideration of whether or not it's worth it to pay.

"But that's just unfair!" you might think. "I'm not in business to give anything away for free!" Well, Blackberries, beepers, and boom-boxes were also cool at one point in history. You can either get on with the times, or spend your career fighting against what is actually going on.

I'm not trying to convince you to give away your services, products, or time away just to make a sale. What I'm showing you is the way people create an expectation of value, and in this book I'll show you how to build this expectation in a way that makes business sense.

When I began my career in the creative field, after giving away designs and ideas for free for "exposure" and trying to gain others' goodwill, I realized first-hand the evils of what we call "spec work." Giving your best value away for free with the expectation of getting paid later is just fooling yourself. It's also a disservice to your own profession, because if you are able to give the best of what you have for free, why would you need to charge anyone in the first place?

Before anyone signs a contract, people want to be convinced that you actually have a solution to their problem, and that your solution is tangible and at their reach. The way they are looking to be convinced isn't through a great sales pitch during the appointment, or right before you try to convince them to close the deal. They need to have a realistic expectation of this valuable solution, formed through first-hand experience.

Think about this gap for a second. You come into a sales appointment with everything valuable about your solution under lock, and the only key to open this lock is the money you receive after a closed sale. You have vowed never to release any value until you get that check. On the other hand, the person on the other side of the table expects value *before* they hand over the check, and until this moment, they have received nothing. They want to feel like they are already moving towards their solution well before they have paid.

What ends up happening when these two mindsets collide is an utter and complete stand-still. Have you ever heard of the paradox of the unstoppable force vs. immovable wall? This is pretty much what is happening here… except that the hiring party says farewell, you lose the sale, and they end up setting an appointment with someone else. Usually, they end up meeting with someone who *does* understand how this expectation of value works and works towards building it ahead of the sales meeting.

GAP #2: FUTILE PERSUASION

Back in an era when communication used to be very slow there weren't too many ways for people to find out about what you could offer them. Unless you both stepped into a physical place at an agreed time with an opportunity to present what you could do for them, there was very little they could know about you ahead of time. Because research and back-and-forth communication used to happen at few and far between moments, the most logical thing to do was to show them an offer and also expect them to make a decision right then and there, while they were sitting in front of us.

There used to be a great pressure to persuade the other party to move forward. Failing to do so would only result in the death of the sale, as it used to be much more difficult to set a second opportunity to meet for further consideration, respond to questions and objections, and continue the wooing process. Often, the person selling would have to begin the presentation from scratch the next time they met, which is a waste of time on everyone's part.

Therefore, the person selling their service felt pressure to close, and this pressure was then passed along to the buying party. The pressure we felt is how we came to hate "pushy salesmen," and in turn, learn to hate the idea of selling altogether.

Our rejection of "pushy" salespeople, along with the fact that buyers can now perform as much research as they want before even coming into contact with you, means that the game has completely changed. The goal used to be to persuade the buyer, yet today, attempting to persuade too directly is seen as a turn-off. Back when we used to play pinball, if you pushed the table too hard, a "TILT" sign came up, the flippers stopped working, and the game was dead. The feeling of these flippers first being completely under your control, and then suddenly feeling the buttons go completely numb, no matter how furiously you pressed them, was the absolute worst. This is exactly how it feels when you fail to realize this gap, decide to push too hard during the sale, and your prospect gets completely turned off.

Now, the new rule is to never persuade directly during the sales appointment. They've performed their research. They've already decided whether they want your solution based on everything they've learned *before* the sales meeting.

Your role today during the sales appointment is to simply clarify and customize your message — which again, they know almost everything about at that point — to their particular circumstance. At that moment, it's more about holding their hand and further deepening the relationship than about starting from scratch presenting your value. The relationship already began long before you stepped into that meeting.

If you're approaching your sales conversations with your value proposition under wraps, you are approaching the issue in a completely wrong manner.

GAP #3: LACK OF INFLUENCE

The third and last gap we'll discuss has to do with what influences a purchase decision. As we saw in the previous point, we used to think that what happened during a sales appointment was the critical factor that determined whether we were going to close or not. Therefore, people in sales pushed to "close hard" so as to not waste this opportunity. We've now learned that people's journey from knowing about us to buying from us has become a lot more complex and extended than this.

The traditional marketing approach was that first, a consumer received a stimulus, which was an impression through some form of media around a product or service. This could be anything from a billboard sign to a brochure.

Based on this stimulus, they would decide to go forth to the point of purchase, or in our case, to the sales appointment. Product packaging, sales presentation process, and other marketing dynamics came into play at this point. The moment they actually purchase the goods and services is what many experts call the First Moment of Truth.

After the consumer made the purchase, they came into the Second Moment of Truth, which is when they experienced what they purchased. For example, they would consume or utilize a product, or experience a service performed. Based on this moment, they would have a first-hand experience of whether what they purchased fulfilled their expectation or not.

A few years ago and based on a vast amount of data across multiple industries, Google came out with an amazing revelation[4] about consumer habits, which has transformed the way we should approach sales. They discovered that in between the Stimulus and the First Moment of Truth lies what they labeled the Zero Moment of Truth, which is where they receive the Stimulus, but perform research to verify whether it is true or not, trustworthy or fake, before considering whether to proceed towards the First Moment of Truth, or the moment of purchase.

This Zero Moment of Truth has proven to be much more of an influential factor than anything that takes place during the initial Stimulus. For a consultative service professional, this means that what you sell before the sales appointment — the *transaction of attention*, which then generates

---

4 *"Winning the Zero Moment of Truth,"* www.thinkwithgoogle.com/marketing-resources/micro-moments/2011-winning-zmot-ebook/

expectation — is going to have a much greater and deeper effect on whether you will be able to succeed during the sales appointment.

The extent to which this has changed the game of selling cannot be taken lightly. Whereas, at one point we thought that our performance and the words spoken *during* the sales appointment were the critical factors that helped close the sale, we have now learned that at that point, we're already late to the game. The most influential moment has already taken place, and this moment now occurs completely outside of our direct control and without our physical presence.

CHAPTER 3

Risks of Not Closing The Gaps

Three Risks

I've shown that these three gaps are based on reality, so failing to address them places you at a severe disadvantage when presenting your offer. Allow me to explain three risks of not closing these gaps.

RISK #1: RESISTANCE

In the previous chapter, we mentioned that a successful Transaction of Attention produces expectation, which then opens the opportunity to make a sale. When we fail to set a proper expectation, it's much more likely that the person on the other end will resist what we are presenting them.

This is just the way we are as human beings. Think about it: nothing that we enjoy in nature is ever processed in the form of sudden flashes that come to us out of nowhere. We interpret things that surprise and jar us without a chance to prepare — think about a bat flying at your face, or a car alarm sounding off in the middle of the night — as unpleasant experiences.

It's just part of our instinctive fight-or-flight response. Our first instinct is to resist abrupt signals. On the other hand, when we have had an opportunity to process them, we are much more open to interpret their meaning and value.

For example, every now and then, I enjoy taking a walk to a park near my house to watch the calm and vast waters of the Tampa Bay, particularly if it's during sunrise or sunset when the colors in the sky change rapidly. The process of walking from my house to the park to observe the scenario is as much a part of the experience as anything.

Now, imagine if I were pleasantly sleeping in my bed at 5:45am, and Scotty from Star Trek decides to beam me up and send me to the park bench right in front of the Bay, how jarring would that be? I would have no time nor mental space to adjust to the new environment.

This illustrates how harsh it feels when you walk into a sales appointment without a prior Transaction of Attention. They are getting in touch with you for the very first time in their lives without a prior expectation of what you're all about. In turn, you are asking for them to process your offer's value, the transaction cost, possible objections, your authority, what makes you different from other alternatives, and every other component of your presentation, without a chance to adjust their mindset from whatever occupied their attention before you started talking.

Given our human nature, the most reasonable thing to do is to put up a resistance. By not closing these gaps, you choose a path that unfortunately reduces your chances of closing the sale.

RISK #2: BURNING YOUR BRAND

Just as closing the Transaction of Attention produces the right expectation, not closing it may emblazon the wrong expectation forever on the consumer's mind. By not working on setting a proper expectation — i.e., your brand — you allow the circumstance to create a random brand for you out of thin air.

Make no mistake, just as you are always selling, you are always creating an impression on others. Whether you want it to or not, this impression becomes your default brand. By not working on improving your brand ahead of time, you place the power to brand yourself in the other person's hands, or worse yet, you let random circumstances brand you.

Let's use attire as an analogy for your personal brand. I'm sure you consider the way you look, the image you're putting forth, as part of the message you're sending when doing business. You take a glance at the jacket you wear, the shoes you select, and the hairstyle that fits the type of business you're looking to present and the type of person you are meeting with. You most likely think about how well your appearance communicates what you want to transmit.

Imagine a scenario in which you attend an appointment to meet with an important executive, and as soon as you show up, the receptionist tells you, "Hi there. Oh, you're here to meet with Mrs. X? Great, please take the clothes on this hanger, and you can go change inside that changing room."

When you look at the hanger, you see clothes you would never wear, much less to a business meeting. The colors are all wrong, and the clothing style just doesn't fit the purpose of your meeting. You naturally balk, but the receptionist says, "Oh you didn't know? Mrs. X gets to select the wardrobe people will wear before meeting with her."

The meeting is so important that you decide to give up your ideas of what best suits your image, and agree to wear those horrible clothes just to meet with this important decision-maker.

Let's say you finish the meeting, and we'll just fast-forward to the follow up email from Mrs. X, where she writes, "Thanks for the great meeting, but we are a bit shocked by the clothes you decided to wear that day, so I don't think we're a good fit to do business."

Sounds completely unfair and ridiculous, doesn't it?

Yet, this is similar to what happens when you haven't made a concerted effort to work on every other aspect of your brand before meeting with someone. You're leaving the way they perceive you up for grabs.

By not defining your personal brand, you let others define it for you.

People receive the wrong expectation of what it means to work with you, because nobody set a proper expectation in the first place.

RISK #3: REPELLING OTHERS

Refusing to close the gaps creates resistance and sets the wrong expectation, but it also pushes others further away from us. This is a problem, because our business depends on connecting with others in a meaningful way.

The reason others move away from us is because, as human beings, we have embedded in our nature, an instinct to flee from the unknown and from perceived threat[5]. We keep our distance from things we don't know enough about. The unknown could be dangerous to ourselves and those we love most and care for. This is a very primitive reaction, but it's something we experience on a daily basis.

The opposite of our natural reaction to distance ourselves from strangers is to be attracted to — or at least open to approach — things we do know. The Transaction of Attention is our best shot at curbing other people's very natural instinct to flee.

Yet, by approaching others without allowing them to have prior knowledge about us, and without impressing a proper expectation upon them, we create a separation between us and the business connections we wish to make with them. This is one reason why cold-calling is widely considered a nuisance. It's why many neighborhoods have laws against door-to-door selling. It's why we've coined the term "junk mail" to refer to messages that were unsolicited.

The most natural reaction to these is to be put off because it's simply fair to know what we're about to invest our attention into. More than just knowing, we want to have assurance that any new experience has a connection with what interests us most at any given moment.

_____

5 "Reactions To Threat And Personality: Psychometric Differentiation Of Intensity And Direction Dimensions Of Human Defensive Behaviour," Perkins AM, Corr PJ., www.ncbi.nlm.nih.gov/pubmed/16406105

THE MOST IMPORTANT BRAND IN THE WORLD

We've just discussed realities about how people react today, and the risks of not adapting our approach to these realities. As you can see, it's very risky to go along and do things the way you've always done them, at least with regard to presenting your value and connecting with others who may want to do business with you.

I've stressed about the importance of forming a proper expectation in others. When you're selling, it's vital for people to know what to expect with regard to the company you represent or the services you offer.

However, if your business requires you to show up face-to-face, on the phone, or even through an online video-conference — in other words, any level of human interaction — then, the expectation of **you** is going to precede the expectation of anything else. If you can't be successful in the Transaction of Attention with regard to *yourself*, it's highly unlikely that people will even care about what you have to say about what you offer.

Your brand is the most important brand in the world, because it is the first one people will come into contact with when doing business with you. The care and attention you place on your personal brand will pay off in a big way. Selling the Brand of **You** is the very first sale you need to close successfully *before* you are able to sell anything else.

> "Selling the Brand of You is the very first sale you need to close successfully before you are able to sell anything else."

We don't normally think about our own brand because we've been told that all we need to do is to represent ourselves behind our company's brand. As much as we care about company brands, we all want to do business with others we know, those with whom we connect with, and those who have gained our trust.

Each gap we've explored, as well as the risks of not closing them, can be overcome by working on your brand. And I mean **your** brand, the Brand of You.

CHAPTER 4

The Mindset Of Building Your Brand

Don't Skip This Chapter

I could continue telling you more about how others buy *you* before they buy *from you*. I could tell you exactly how to show up in the best light. I could show you the *exact* steps you need to take to develop your personal brand.

Yet, none of this would matter if you resist the idea that from now on, your main professional focus above anything else is to work on developing the Brand of You.

If you're looking to make a difference in your profession, open the door to more opportunities, close more sales, and have more happy clients, you must work on developing the Brand of **You.**

In this chapter, we'll go through eight negative beliefs that might be blocking you from taking this important step forward, with some tips on how to destroy those obstacles. We'll also look at a few other positive tips to build your brand on the most solid foundation.

Nine Deadly Lies

Let me share a secret with you: I've fought against feelings of insecurity my whole life. I was never the popular kid in school. I was the skinny, dorky kid that would use up his recess time playing the piano inside the teachers' lounge, while everyone else in the playground was fully focused on being cool.

Although I did what made me happy, I was haunted by feelings of inadequacy and the fear of missing out. I wondered whether I'd be happier if I just became one of them. These feelings have continued chasing me all the way to the present, and I often need to make a conscious effort to put those aside and show up the way I know I should. I can discuss these obstacles because I've personally dealt with all of them.

I completely understand if you have doubts about whether it's a good idea to raise your profile in your industry. I would dare to say that at some point or another, you've had to confront one of the following nine deadly lies:

1. "I'm not an expert."
2. "I'm not the best."
3. "Nobody is making money."
4. "I'm broke."
5. "I don't have enough time."
6. "I'm not worth that much."
7. "It's someone else's fault."

8. "There's too much competition."
9. "It's not the right time yet."

If you dig deep inside, you'll be able to pinpoint the exact statement that's causing you to think twice about standing up for the value you can bring to your industry. These are lies, or at the very least, severe misunderstandings about your reality.

Let's look at each one in detail, along with some thoughts on how to deal with them.

DEADLY LIE #1: "I'M NOT AN EXPERT."

When thinking about your personal brand, you might have hesitated to develop it because you don't feel like you're enough of an expert to stand up and represent your industry. This is born from the false idea that only "experts" — whatever that term might mean — deserve to stand up as a source of ideas, insights, and service to others.

Let's first look at the concept of an "expert." In most fast-moving industries, anyone in your field who you might regard as an expert is only a week or two away from falling behind the times. This is why these "experts" consume content about their field voraciously. They know that their expertise isn't something they carry inherently, but rather, a skill acquired as a consequence of their constant effort to keep updated.

> "To people needing your services, integrity and humility are so much more important than seeing you as an expert."

What does this tell you? It means that you can probably catch up to the times by consuming the latest about your industry. I'm not saying that you'll become an expert in a couple of weeks; however, if you're serious about becoming confident, you will be amazed at how much you can accelerate your knowledge by reading a few good books and spending a good number of hours on solid YouTube channels.

Aside from this, you really do not have to be an expert to stand up boldly as someone who can help others. You do have to have integrity that you understand what you're prescribing to others and enough humility to recognize when you don't know enough to respond to a particular question. To people needing your services, integrity and humility are so much more important than seeing you as an expert, so strive for that and don't worry too much about being the "expert".

Takeaways

- Experts are people who have had more exposure to information than the majority.
- Even experts can fall behind the times.
- You can catch up by informing yourself properly.
- Integrity and humility are more valuable than expertise.

DEADLY LIE #2: "I'M NOT THE BEST."

This one is similar to the negative belief we just discussed. You might feel like you're not a member of the elite group of pros who seem to have success in everything they do.

In reality, no member of that fictional elite group *really* thinks they're the best in their industry, but they sure as heck *show up as if they were.*

I know people who have worked in my field for a longer period than I have. They've attended better schools than I have. They have also had more prestigious job experiences than I have. These factors actually don't matter one bit when it comes time to express my convictions about a subject related to my field, and this is true for two main reasons:

1. Because I will always give what I truly believe is the correct answer, without seeking anybody else's approval (waiting for someone else's approval has slowed me down too many times and will slow you down as well).

2. Because I have zero fear of being wrong, and being corrected doesn't hurt my ego anymore — which is what fuels point number 1 above.

On the other hand, people don't always hire services from "the very best" in an industry. Most people are quite content to hire someone who is awesome at what they do, regardless of how many gold plaques or diamond rings or whatever other silliness they might have decorating the walls of their office.

> *"Your job isn't to be the best in your industry; it's to be the very best version of yourself that you can be."*

Your job isn't to be the best in your industry; it's to be the very best version of yourself that you can be. Stop comparing yourself to others, and just compare yourself with where you were last week. Are you on the path towards improving yourself? If so, great. You're on the right track.

Takeaways

- Showing up as the best is more effective than trying to *be* the best.

- You should work on clarifying your stance on industry topics and expressing them boldly.

- Don't be afraid of being wrong and admitting so when you are indeed wrong. This shows that you honor the truth.

- People don't often look to hire the best. They are looking for someone who knows their stuff.

DEADLY LIE #3: "NOBODY IS MAKING MONEY."

This statement keeps you down when you wonder whether it's even worth putting in the effort to rise in your field. When looking forward to the end goal, you might not see enough of a reward on the other side.

It might be very difficult to make a living in your field. For all I know, someone reading this book is stuck in the 1950's and is still going door to door selling vacuum cleaners. If it's *actually* true that nobody in your field is making money, then it might be time to seriously consider a career change.

Still, many people *feel* like nobody in their industry is making money, even though some people in their field are indeed doing quite well. This feeling of scarcity is usually a result of being in an industry where too many people are competing for a small slice of business, although none of them offer anything unique that differentiates them from the next.

If this is the case in your field, then it's probably not that there is a scarcity of business; the real truth might be that there is no money to be earned by those who are content selling their services in the exact same manner as everyone else.

Breaking the pattern of showing up just like everyone else does is exactly what I'll be discussing in the next few chapters, so rather than going any deeper into breaking this myth, I'll just ask you to keep reading.

Takeaways

- If you are in a dying industry, you might need to give up and change careers.

- If you are in a commoditized industry, you need to work on standing out.

- People who follow the masses are missing out on the rewards. This happens in every field.

DEADLY LIE #4: "I'M BROKE."

It's often the case that we don't show up boldly because we haven't yet achieved a reasonable level of financial success. *If only our bank accounts were overflowing, we would stand firmly for what we believe.* It would be the perfect evidence that we are the ones to trust...or so we are led to believe.

Thinking this way is just like putting the cart before the horse. You might have bought into the idea that financial success is a sign that others approve of your value, and that you need this approval to show up more confidently. This deadly lie is like saying "People won't like what I can provide them because they haven't liked it before now."

The reason why you haven't achieved financial success very well may be because you haven't placed yourself in the market as a valuable solution to other people's problems. I've known many skilled and talented professionals who go through periods of scarcity, but have brushed it off and consistently kept presenting value to others, and have overcome times of adversity.

Unless you're selling "Get Rich Quick" schemes — and if so, shame on you! — people are not really looking at your financial status before they buy from you. They're more interested in whether you have a valuable solution to their problems, and whether you are the right person to deliver this solution.

> *"Whatever happened before in your life, you can just turn the page and call today a new beginning."*

You need to stop thinking that you need to have gotten other people's stamp of approval to close more deals.

Whatever happened before in your life, you can just turn the page and call today a new beginning.

Takeaways

- Past failures don't determine future success. If this were so, it would be impossible to grow.

- If you haven't yet stood up in your field as a valuable problem-solver, you can't really judge from your results.

- People are interested in finding valuable solutions, and people with integrity who can implement them.

- You don't need to carry stamps of approval to present your value.

DEADLY LIE #5: "I DON'T HAVE ENOUGH TIME."

Complaining about not having enough time to do what we know needs to get done is pretty common in our day, especially with our currency of attention in such short supply. If you're like me, this is the default excuse I come up with whenever something isn't getting done.

> *"You have the same available hours as the President, celebrities, and the highest-earning individuals in your field."*

The truth of the matter is that each of us wakes up with the exact same amount of time as everyone else. You have the same available hours as the President, celebrities, and the highest-earning individuals in your field. It's one of the few instances in our reality in which no matter how rich or poor you are, no matter what country you live in nor what conditions surround you, we all have the same amount of this valuable resource available to us. Saying that you don't have time makes absolutely zero sense.

Every single person who has done something noteworthy has employed their time in a manner that is a bit more productive than the average human being.

The truth about this complaint lies in what it reveals: that you haven't decided to focus on working on a particular task. The most common reason you don't work on something is that you haven't made it a priority. It's better to come clean and admit that you haven't worked on something because it's just not important enough for you, than to blame outside circumstances you have no control over, such as the rotation of the Earth or how quickly your clock ticks.

It is amazing what you can accomplish by waking up an hour earlier, going to bed an hour later, or dedicating one less hour to entertainment each day. I'm not at all against entertainment, relaxing, and recreation; yet, a reality of our culture is that we've placed way too much importance on being entertained. In fact, the average American spends over 5 hours each day on TV, leisure, and sports (compare that to about 9 hours each day spent on sleeping)[6]. That's ⅓ of each day spent on distractions…and these are usually the same people complaining that they don't have time!

The easiest action to take in order to "find more time" is to swap out one entertainment activity for an action related to working on your brand. Be objective, specific, and intentional about it. For example, you can swap out a daily one-hour episode of CSI:Saskatchewan for one hour writing an article. Once you do this a few times, and begin receiving the rewards for doing so, spending your time wisely will become a habit that supports your growth.

Takeaways

- Everyone has the exact same amount of time available.

- Saying you don't have time is a lie and an excuse for not prioritizing.

- As a quick action to find more time, look entertainment activities you invest time into, and swap a few out for something that will help you build your brand.

DEADLY LIE #6: "I'M NOT WORTH THAT MUCH."

Many professionals around the world suffer from a deep-seated fear— and it's not the fear of failure, but the exact opposite: the fear of success. Within yourself, you wholeheartedly believe that you don't deserve to be richly compensated, nor regarded for the work you perform.

When you believe this lie and you're right at the fringe of a great opportunity, an amazing connection, or a multiple-digit paycheck, you feel paralyzed, dirty, and inadequate. This stops you from seeking out more of these opportunities, as you feel you need to avoid the guilt of squandering them.

---

6 American Time Use Survey, from the Bureau of Labor Statistics, bls.gov/tus

Here's the truth: You're never worth as much as you *want* to be worth, but neither are you worth as little as you think you are. Your value as a professional comes from the market. In other words, you're worth what others are willing to pay you for your services.

> "You have the ability to influence how much other people value you, based on how boldly you show up."

Now, here's the good news: You have the ability to influence how much other people value you, based on how boldly you show up. You don't have to wait passively for others to put a price tag on you. The best way to get what you're worth is to represent yourself as if you're worth that much.

I've experienced this first-hand many times throughout my career. Whether I think I'm not worth much, or I think I deserve to be compensated highly, people around me seem to "magically" agree! It's not that I'm sending off telepathic signals about my self-appraisal. Others can somehow sense what I think I'm worth through the way I speak, the words I choose, the boldness with which I express my ideas, my body language, and other ways I communicate my value to them.

All of this flows from my deep conviction that I am a highly valuable asset to whomever decides to engage in business with me.

If you read that last sentence and thought it sounded a bit arrogant, stop for a bit and ask yourself if it's fair to interpret confidence as arrogance. You might think that it is arrogant of you to think highly about yourself, but if so, you must fight this limiting belief.

If you sincerely think you have a valuable solution to other people's issues, and can deliver this solution with passion and integrity, there is absolutely no reason why you should think about yourself as anything less than who you are. In fact, presenting yourself as anything less than your actual value would be lying to others, as you're failing to deliver what could really help them under the pretense of some false humility you've felt you needed to have.

You are worth more. The fact that you are reading this book shows that you are willing to invest into yourself and act upon your actual value.

For the next day, practice thinking that you are a highly valuable asset. Even if you don't really believe it just yet. For now, just pretend this is who you are. Pay attention to how others react to your self-confidence and observe the difference it makes in the way they react toward you.

Takeaways

- Recognize whether you have fear of success, so you can deal with it.

- Your value is assigned by the market, but you can influence the market by the bold way you show up.

- Diminishing your value robs other people from the solution that you can implement in their lives and their businesses, and is ultimate unfair to them.

- Practice thinking of yourself as a highly-valuable asset and observe the difference it makes.

DEADLY LIE #7: "IT'S SOMEONE ELSE'S FAULT."

This one was suggested by a good friend of mine and I wasn't even thinking about including it. It's so pervasive and difficult to detect, but so easy to ignore.

Sometimes, we stay completely stuck due to something that happened to us. It could be a bad business partnership, being laid off of a job, someone taking unfair advantage of us, or anything else that puts us in a negative slump. We tell ourselves that we would have moved forward, if only someone wouldn't have done this or that.

Whatever happened to you *may* have been someone else's fault, but the fault for staying stuck at this moment is entirely your own — and I'm very sorry if it hurts you to hear this, but it's the truth!

Whatever they did to you has very little to do with how you decide to process the lesson learned and apply it to your life.

Your ego might be hurt a bit by accepting responsibility, but I promise that this pain goes away quickly. It's like ripping a bandage off of your skin; it stings for a bit, but then the cool breeze soothes it off.

When you accept responsibility, you also recognize that you're in control of your situation. You can take a step forward if you want to. The only reason you wouldn't do so is because you didn't think *you could*, but now you know you can.

Sometimes, it even helps to think about it as a challenge that this person has presented you with. They are betting on your failure, so will you prove them right? Or will you succeed in the face of the challenge? Mind you, I don't think it's healthy to think you'll one day get a chance to rub your success in their face. Just let that go.

Think about it as a game you're playing against an imaginary opponent. You can put that person's face on your opponent as a mask, but you're not really competing against anyone else. When you succeed, it's not about the way others lose, but just about you breaking through the obstacle.

Takeaways

- A bad situation may be someone else's fault.
- Choosing to remain stuck because of it is entirely our responsibility.
- We can control our situation by accepting responsibility and moving on.
- Think about it as a game you're playing against an imaginary opponent, and let go of the actual person who may have affected you.

DEADLY LIE #8: "THERE'S TOO MUCH COMPETITION."

One reason we tend to stay put without moving forward is because we perceive that there is just too much competition, and we'd rather not deal with the ferocious battle of doing business. Most people avoid conflict, so feeling like it's going to take a set of plated armor and a two-handed sword to go out and get business shocks us into inaction.

The underlying idea behind this fear is that business is so scarce that there are going to be thousands of people picking away at the same accounts, prospects, or projects. There are three issues around this kind of thinking.

First, it is absolutely not true that there is no potential business to be earned *as long as there is a market for what you are offering.* People around the world are happy to pay for well-performed services, and if what you offer is valuable, then more than likely, there is enough business to go around and not enough competitors to take on the whole market.

The second issue around thinking this way is that you are approaching business like a battle, and not as an opportunity to offer your unique solutions. I used to think this way as well. My thought was that my advancement depended on getting the deals before anyone else could. So, naturally, I was highly protective and even a bit paranoid. I experienced that the business I was paranoid about getting was never worth it. On the contrary, the business that flowed to me organically — as a result of raising my profile — always turned into my best clients.

The third and last issue with this way of thinking is precisely what I just mentioned. It really isn't worth it to stress about getting ahead of competitors, because that type of attitude breeds the worst kind of clients. As a result of working on your personal brand, you will immediately differentiate yourself among other providers. Any energy you used to spend on worrying about other people nibbling away at your pie, you should now spend on moving forward and advancing your own game. The way to "defeat competition" isn't to fight against them, but rather, to make yourself so visible and unique that the most outstanding solution your prospects see in their minds is the one *you* offer.

Takeaways

- The concern around competition comes from a mindset of scarcity.

- More than likely, there is plenty of business to go around.

- You shouldn't approach business as a battle against competitors, but rather, an opportunity to offer your unique solutions to people and businesses that need it.

- The business people fight for isn't business you really want. It is much more enjoyable to do business with clients who come as a result of being attracted by your personal brand.

DEADLY LIE #9: "IT'S NOT THE RIGHT TIME."

I almost forgot this one, but a friend suggested that I include it and she was totally right. I've been set backwards so many times because I didn't feel like it was the right time to take action.

Don't get me wrong. I do believe many critical decisions hinge on waiting for the right time. The reason I'm including this among our list of lies is because most times we state it, timing actually has nothing to do with the circumstances.

We're often dazed under the illusion that there is a "perfect time" to do everything. You have to be completely ready, every detail needs to be perfect, and you need to be 100% together before you can pursue opportunities.

Total lies! Imperfect action will beat perfect inaction every single time.

> "Imperfect action will beat perfect inaction every single time."

Furthermore, when you do take action despite feeling like it's the wrong time, you are bound to learn many valuable lessons, and it will help you perfect your approach.

Instead of taking one giant step whenever the "perfect time" arrives, you can get wherever you want to by taking incremental small steps in the right direction. If your next step forward is too drastic to take now, it's OK to think about taking a less riskier action, as long as you're not compromising your momentum. In other words, don't fool yourself into doing something that won't really contribute towards advancing your cause.

I don't really believe we should dwell in our "What if's," but sometimes I look back at the things I've achieved to see if I could have done it any better. For anything I've accomplished, I'm convinced that I could have begun much sooner and everything would have been fine.

Maybe if I had not waited for the "perfect time," I would have even been much farther in my career. I would've built my company sooner, developed more products, written more books, and helped many more people.

Today I'm highly motivated to avoid the regret of not moving forward. I can deal with not doing things in a "perfect" manner, as it'll result in lessons learned and experience gained. But the pain of having lost precious time is sharp and can never be recovered.

There is no "perfect time". Your *tomorrow-you* will thank your *present-you* for taking action now.

Takeaways

- The "perfect time" to take action is often an illusion.

- Taking imperfect action is more effective than waiting to take perfect action.

- Most decisions can be made sooner than you feel is right, which more than likely will bring results quicker. At the very least, you'll learn some valuable lessons.

- Motivate yourself by avoiding the regret of not moving forward.

No More Lies

I hope that by exposing these lies, and offering tips to deal with them, you can promise yourself that you will no longer use them as an excuse. Especially when it comes to working on your own brand, it really makes no sense for you to become an obstacle for your own growth!

You Are Here To Help

One of the reasons it is so important for you to take action and work on your personal brand is that at this very moment, there are thousands and thousands of people who are suffering from the exact problem that you are equipped to solve.

I don't care if *you* feel that what you do is easy. They certainly don't see it that way. They see their problem as highly difficult and complex, and they are willing to pay someone like you to just get rid of it and help them get on with their lives or their business. If they thought it was easy, they would've solved it themselves a long time ago.

A headstrong mindset towards sincerely helping others will work like a huge hammer to break through the deadly little lies, the obstacles and false beliefs, the lack of confidence, and anything else holding you back. It will also help you position yourself as a means to deliver the solution that people desperately need.

You need to invest everything into the goal of helping others. Any significant and steady advancement you make won't come as a result of grabbing away at what you feel you want, but rather, by giving others what they need.

Your personal brand is just a sign that you're clear on how exactly you can solve these problems and who you can solve them for. It's the furthest thing from a cheap way to pump your ego.

If you were crawling through the desert under a scorching sun, in dire thirst, and you saw a stand with a sign that says "COLD WATER," you would never say, "I would've bought the water if only that sign weren't so bold and arrogant." You would actually *thank* the person in the stand for clearly displaying the solution you were desperately looking for, and in such a way that it was impossible to ignore.

This is exactly what happens when you clarify your brand. People who *do need you* will appreciate the fact that you showed up and gave them relief that their problem had a solution.

The Unending Struggle Against Ego

One of the main points of resistance people have against developing their personal brand is that they perceive it as an exercise to pump up their ego. Nobody wants to feel like they're the arrogant, cocky, big-headed figure within their circle of friends and colleagues.

As a result of this fear, they take on an attitude where they sort of hide and just "let things occur organically." Instead of standing up and clarifying what they can do for others, they wait until someone chooses them.

In the meantime, they just occupy their time and attention on trivial matters, like funny memes, the latest TV show, political banter, or sports.

The reality, however, is that ego is *always* in play. It's even a factor in people that have this supposedly "humble" attitude.

Think about it: These people hide their value because they're afraid of what people might think about them. In other words, they're more concerned about *their image* rather than about clarifying how they can serve others. They're more concerned about keeping their value, their knowledge, and their advice all to themselves, rather than promoting themselves as someone who can provide the help other people need. They're counting on other people remembering their name, and fishing them out from a sea of competitors, without any effort on their part to speak about what they do nor what authority they have. Think about how arrogant *that* is!

It doesn't matter if you promote yourself or you don't. Ego is always something that you'll have to battle against. To me, this means that the struggle against ego has absolutely nothing to do with developing a personal brand or not.

And if the struggle against ego is always there, why wouldn't you consider developing your brand so you can help more people and move further along in your business?

Being The Trusted Source of Knowledge

One responsibility you take on when developing your personal brand is that you establish yourself as a channel of information for people who may have questions about your field. You're there to shed light on obscure or confusing topics within your field, and you respond to people's questions with empathy, but also with authority.

Many people with whom I have personal and business relationships come to me in moments when they have doubts about my topic of expertise. They know they can come to me whenever they have questions, and they know they won't get the answer that they could have Googled on their own, but rather, a highly passionate, empathetic, and relevant response.

In the process of developing your brand, you will notice that you will naturally establish yourself as a source of information for others. You will be taking on a huge responsibility, as telling people where to go and what to do is something to be taken very seriously. Yet, it is highly rewarding. You are standing up as the source of reference for people who are wondering what to do in their time of need.

As you become the trusted source of knowledge, you will also be required to inform yourself and be totally immersed in your field. You can't afford to merely speak from theory, nor from your gut the whole time. You must be armed with research, facts, and practical experiences on what works and what doesn't. Only in this manner, can you warn people about making a costly mistake, or point them towards success.

Developing Passion

The last element we'll discuss about the mindset of your personal brand is passion. People might be convinced that you are skilled enough to provide what they need, but what will really convince them that you are the right person to provide the service is that you are deeply passionate about what you do.

If you think of your profession as simply something you do to get money to pay for your groceries or your mortgage, people will sense your lack of enthusiasm and interpret it as a lack of commitment on your part.

When people are looking for a solution, they want to know that the person solving it can do so effectively, but they also want to be sure that if anything in the process goes wrong — for example, if a project gets delayed, or if an unexpected situation occurs — that whomever is providing the service is devoted enough to seek a way to reach the goal. They want to know that you are committed to seeing the process through until the end, no matter what it takes. Someone who is just in it for money to buy stuff will simply give up as soon as the going gets rough.

Another quality of passionate professionals is that they feed on the latest developments in their industry, and do so on a frequent basis. They are constantly on the lookout for better, faster, and more cost-efficient ways to produce results. To them, this isn't a chore. Consuming information about their industry is something they fully enjoy, just as they might enjoy other forms of recreation and entertainment.

As a result of actively consuming insights about their space, from every end of the spectrum and from multiple viewpoints, they develop their own thoughts, feelings, and opinions about what's going on in their field. They've developed their own balanced and defined thoughts on what really works today. Back when they were just entering the field, they might have made lots of references to other people's opinions, but after two or three years, they are able to clearly express their stance on the past, present, and future of their industry.

This is only possible when you are passionately invested in your professional field.

Would you sit down after a hard day of work, and relax by reading magazines or content sites about your industry, without considering it "work"? Would you put up a poster about terminology in your field on your office wall, just as if it were a piece of art? Would you attend an industry conference on your vacation time, and feel like your time was well spent? Would you dedicate a coffee break to connect with someone who does the exact same work as you, and enjoy sharing tips and tricks on how you manage to help your clients?

None of this is crazy if you are in love with what you do and are deeply passionate about helping others. Get immersed in what originally made you passionate about your field, and add on to that the future smiles from people you will be able to support by just doing what you love.

Final Thoughts About Mindset

I struggled a lot with whether to include this chapter in the book, as I thought it could come across as too "self-help-ish." To be honest, this chapter wasn't even in my original outline for the book.

The more I talked to people while preparing the content for the book, the more I realized that these mindset issues cripple people from taking significant steps forward in their profession, just as they've done to me in the past. No matter how much sound advice I share throughout the rest of the book, it would all be useless if I didn't first deal with that annoying internal voice which rejects any help I could offer.

You know which voice I'm talking about: the voice constantly yammering about in your head with those little lies we just went over. It's the voice fooling you into wasting your time and overlooking opportunities.

I hope these tips have revealed limiting ideas that may have been holding you back, and that once you can identify them, you can begin taking steps to put them aside and never allow them to stand in your way again.

CHAPTER 5

Four Main Challenges When Establishing a Brand

Here Come The Challenges...

A few chapters back, we established that the Transaction of Attention is followed by expectation, which is followed by a Second Transaction, which we typically call "a closing" at the sales appointment. We've also seen that the most reasonable way to set the right expectation in advance is by developing our personal brand.

In other eras we identified whether our business was B2B (Business to Business) or B2C (Business to Consumer), today's speed of communication has made P2P — Person to Person — the default means to exchange business value. This is why setting a proper expectation about yourself as a person is as important — and in many cases even *more* important — as the company brand that you are looking to represent.

You have probably heard people say something similar to, "I wasn't so sure about buying this or that, but I just kind of liked the guy." Liking someone isn't so much about having good charms, being lucky, or being a runner-up at a beauty contest. If you're looking to generate affinity, it has everything to do with how confident you are about yourself and the value you personally offer. It's also about how well you are able to project this value in person and through other elements of your personal brand, which people get into contact with before getting in direct contact with you.

As I mentioned in our previous chapter, some people resist the idea of a personal brand, as the concept might feel impersonal, cold, and pretentious to them. I understand the resistance, as I myself was unsure about this idea for a long period of time. I used to think it was better to just let things be, and let the pieces fall where they may.

The problem is, pieces *do* fall where they will but in most cases when we don't develop our personal brand, they fall in random places. In many of those cases, our personal brand is forged by circumstances and situations fully outside of our control, and we end up affected by the gaps we've already explored throughout the previous chapters.

Now, I'll assume at this point that you are fully convinced that you must work on developing your personal brand, and let's say you're ready to begin working. You might be completely clear about your goal, and you understand how solidifying your personal brand could help you grow your business.

I've met many people who are fully convinced that this is what they need to do, and they have dedicated an enormous amount of time, energy, and resources on their personal brand, yet are unfortunately hindered by a number of very real obstacles, which I'll detail for you throughout this chapter.

Because these obstacles are in their way, their personal brand never supports their business in the way they originally set out to. It's a bit like investing a good sum of money to purchase an expensive battery-powered tool but because it's actually missing the battery, it ends up not helping you with the job you needed to get done. Was it the tool's fault? Was it your mistake for choosing the tool? Of course not. The fact that the tool was incomplete means that it *could've* gotten the job done, but it didn't do so because of its incompleteness.

In the same way, a personal brand may be limited by one or more of these challenges. Many professionals set out to develop their authority, yet end up frustrated because it ends up doing nothing to help their business.

I want you to be absolutely clear on the pitfalls you need to avoid as you develop a brand that represents you, sets the right expectation, and which you can use as leverage to close more sales and grow your business.

First Challenge: Synthetic

Many times, people who pay attention to a brand end up becoming disillusioned and walking away after they realize the brand was just an artificial front, built only to hook people's attention in a cheap manner. There's no space for deeper engagement because their personal brand was just too shallow.

I call this an issue of being *Synthetic*.

I remember one time I was about to eat some plastic apples we had as decoration in our house. They *looked* so nice and juicy, and they certainly were attractive! The plastic apples were carefully designed to look edible and attract the eye. Yet, when I reached out to pick one up, there was no weight to it and it felt hard and "plasticky." The truth that it was a fake apple traveled through my fingertips, up to my brain, and straight to my disappointment. Good thing I didn't go so far as to bite into it!

The same thing happens when a personal brand looks good from far away, but has zero substance. The consumer's reaction tends to be similar to how I felt about the plastic apple. The realization may take a bit longer, because the fact that it's a synthetic brand may not be apparent right away, but believe me, people do figure it out. We all get disappointed when we find out there is no substance offered.

Can you think about a celebrity who gave an impression of having one kind of personality, and then through some unfortunate life event, they show their true colors? Or a preacher who is unveiled to be corrupt and twisted after a scandal? Or how about a corporate leader who supposedly aligns with the company's mission and values, only for you to find out that their lives are completely out of line with what they are supposed to stand for?

These are classic examples of Synthetic personal brands. These people were never *really* who they pretended to be. The brand people were attracted toward was never there to begin with. It was all an illusion, an avatar built to manipulate people. It is the very definition of being *fake*.

The result of a personal brand being Synthetic is an issue of depth. People can't build a deeper relationship with the person they were attracted to because there really was no depth to that person. Therefore, that brand only served to attract on a superficial level, but hardly ever stands scrutiny to allow real business to take place. People seek to do business with other people they like, but what do you think happens when they discover that the person they liked doesn't even exist?

A Synthetic brand also affects longevity. Here I'm referring to how long people are willing to be connected to that brand by paying their attention. A Synthetic personal brand may not sustain enough attention to generate interest towards a sale, because people get turned off and disappointed well before any such conversation is even possible.

Worse yet, in the event that it *does* generate a transaction of value in exchange for money, an even more disastrous situation might take place. If people like someone enough to hand over their money, yet afterwards, find out that they've just been dealing with a mask and not a true person, this might lead to refunds, cancellations, and sometimes even legal action.

It's wrong and even immoral to dupe people into purchasing something under false pretenses. If we were talking about everyday product brands, we would call this "false advertising." I am fully convinced that showing up as someone you are not is another example of false advertising.

SYNTHETIC VS. AUTHENTIC

People are usually willing to pay attention to those who are not showing up as a contrived character built to manipulate, but rather, as someone true to the essence of who they actually are.

Why does it seem like being authentic is so difficult for some people? The allure of building a fake character for themselves is probably based on their dreams of attracting droves of followers and large audiences, but as we've seen, this isn't really sustainable. The appearance doesn't last long and it can backfire — as it often does. The disappointment people experience can often be impossible to repair and will not only leave you with unhappy relationships and clients, but a damaged reputation as well. Being authentic can be like an insurance policy against causing this type of disappointment.

This is an issue I've had to deal with during the past decade or so. Laser-quick bio: I was born in New York City, and at seven years of age, was dropped in the Dominican Republic knowing hardly any Spanish. This was at first very confusing, but little by little I adapted to my parents' culture. After many years of living, studying, and working in the D.R., I "immigrated" back to the United States, and was forced to "re-learn" English and how to live here. I not only became fully bilingual, but I also became "bicultural" — meaning that I am culturally neither American nor Dominican, but some weird blend in-between. I can shift easily between my two cultures, but I can't remain on one side for too long. What I just described *is* my authentic self.

I've had to wrestle with the temptation to conform to what most people around me expect, given that I don't easily "fit in." For example, I'm terrible with slang — in either language — and I can't pick up sarcasm very easily. I constantly feel like people look at me and think "Just be yourself…but also be a bit more like this other guy."

The easiest way to fail at closing the Transaction of Attention is to be just like everyone else. Do you remember that scene in The Matrix — don't lie, you've watched it a million times — where Neo and Morpheus are walking among a crowded city, everyone is dressed in black and gray, and suddenly the lady dressed in red walks by? Neo couldn't resist paying attention, and Morpheus jumped on this closed Transaction of Attention to bring expectation ("Were you listening to me, Neo? Or were you looking at the woman in the red dress?") and then took his attention to reveal the gran lesson: his mind-blowing revelation of how the Matrix works.

The lady in the red dress was a perfect cinematographic technique used to symbolize one thing that stands out among a crowd due to being drastically distinct. Many of us might struggle to be unique, as we're so close to our own selves that we fail to see anything exciting or out of the norm about who we are.

Here's the simple secret to a unique personal brand: it needs to be grounded upon who you really are. There might be a hundred thousand other people in your line of profession, yet none who embody the exact same values and aspects as you, nor have the same life story, strengths, and flaws as you have.

On top of all this, it is highly unlikely that there are many people with your exact same style and approach towards topics in your field. Maybe you don't think you have a style, but believe me, you do. Everyone does. Even through words you use when you send a text message from your phone, your style can be on full display.

There's a high possibility that you've never paid attention to these elements about yourself. You may have wondered how to be unique, but maybe you had never heard that the secret to achieve a unique style is much easier than you thought.

Developing a personal brand grounded on who you actually are isn't as simple as "being yourself." In some way or another, you can't help being yourself. The goal is to *express* who you actually are *through* your personal brand, instead of embracing a brand that could very well belong to anyone else. (We'll dive more into this, beginning with the next chapter.)

Consider your authentic answers to these questions:

- What moves you to talk about your business?
- Can I really trust you?
- Are you truly who you say you are?
- Do you have an authentic, indisputable reason for doing business?

Second Challenge: Obscurity

A popular quote goes, "if a tree falls in a forest and nobody's around to hear it, does it make a sound?" In a similar manner, if you have a personal brand, but nobody ever comes into contact with it, do you really have a personal brand?

Your brand is only relevant to the degree that it is able to connect with others, and ideally, with the audience that will most likely want to do business with you.

Yet, people still find themselves developing a personal brand that ends up in utter obscurity. You can't find them mentioned anywhere when inquiring about specialists in a certain topic. You often can't even find some of these people when searching for *them* either! Their personal brand probably requires someone to climb into their heads to see what they're about, because as far as the external world, it's as present as a T-Rex shopping along the streets of Paris.

Given that the Transaction of Attention requires something for them to *pay attention* to, obscurity can be a disastrous setback towards this goal. How many people would give money to buy something mysterious hidden under a tablecloth? We know the concept of placing goods on display for others to see and to consider a purchase. Stores place their most attractive products in their windows, and their websites place their featured products on their front page. This exact same dynamic occurs with people selling their services. When people are interested in what we can offer them, they need to be able to locate us without much trouble or effort.

CAN I FIND YOU EASILY?

Defeating obscurity is about being found easily by the right person at the right time. If it takes a tremendous amount of effort to reach someone that can help me, then something is not quite right. Furthermore, if I'm the one that needs to make an effort to find you, it casts doubt on whether you are even the right person to talk to.

I'm not saying that your personal brand needs to reach celebrity levels of popularity and recognition for it to be an asset for your business. The goal here isn't to be as massively popular as a recognized figure like Justin Bieber or Rihanna, but rather, to be found easily by the right person and at the right time.

Who am I talking about when I say "the right person"? I'm referring to the people looking to do business and looking to acquire what we're offering. "The right time" means when it matters the most *to them*, right when they are looking for solutions to their problems and are open to being sold to.

BEING "EVERYWHERE"

Personal brands that have defeated obscurity are those which appear to be everywhere — everywhere that matters, that is. Wherever people go to find out how to solve their problems, they are bound to come across elements of that person's brand as they exchanged value for attention and began a relationship with them.

Being in all places sounds a whole lot more difficult than it actually is. There is no need to attend every single networking event, book your whole calendar with meetings, be on Twitter all day, or tell your pitch to everyone who passes by at the corner of a busy city. Even without taking these somewhat extreme actions, a strong personal brand manages to get found and will attract the right people.

I can't tell you the number of people that come into contact with me, usually through an email or a private chat, to tell me that they've found out about me and have been following me for a while before deciding to reach out. Some have even thanked me for the way I've helped them, before I ever had a chance to talk to them, or even meet them in person!

The reason this happens is that my personal brand, and the assets that support it, work on my behalf, whether I am physically present or not. By following the recommendations I'm sharing with you throughout this book, you'll create an extension of yourself that is more far-reaching than you could ever accomplish by only relying on the very little you can do when you're physically present.

OBSCURE VS. ATTRACTIVE

On the surface, the opposite of obscurity would be "visibility." So far, we've talked about the importance of *being found*, so it's natural to think that the alternative to being obscure would be to just be *more visible*.

In such a crowded and noisy world as ours, merely being visible is not enough. A single bee is just as visible as the thousand other bees in the beehive. It doesn't mean that a single bee becomes invisible just because they are lost between a swarm of other bees. The illusion occurs because despite being visible, a single bee can't stand out from the massive swarm.

A personal brand that can be found, but is just the same as everyone else, certainly doesn't suffer from invisibility; it suffers from a lack of appeal. It's an unfortunate problem which causes it to not draw the attention of people who matter. The Transaction of Attention never takes place because their brand isn't on display in a manner that appeals or motivates people to make this investment.

Investing in being visible is easy. Media — even social media — is now a pay-for-play game. Racking up impressions for your brand is just a direct result of how much money you have available to spend, but this doesn't really move you any further. It's not about how much money you have available to burn on advertising, nor is it about how many "eyeballs" you get to look at you.

An attractive brand is not only about showing up in front of people, but also about motivating them to get closer and listen in. It's about closing the Transaction of Attention. You make paying attention to you a no-brainer, and your brand connects so deeply with their interests that the attraction becomes irresistible.

In chapter 7, I discuss exactly what goes into developing an attractive personal brand, and how you can improve this trait for your own brand.

Some questions worth asking about your brand:

- Can I find you easily (offline or online)?

- Are you "everywhere"?

- Are you just hidden in plain sight?

- If so, what can you do to change that?

Third Challenge: Irrelevant

T he next problem that really weighs down on building a solid personal brand is irrelevancy. In too many cases, someone manages to become visible, attractive, and authentic. So far, so good. However, the goal of building our brand isn't to be a celebrity with a long line of fans and followers, but to support and grow our businesses. It's not merely about drawing in eyeballs, but to catch the attention of those who are clear on what we offer so that they may talk to others about us.

The problem with those building an irrelevant personal brand is that these people may become known, but not necessarily for what they do. People know *who* they are, yet hardly ever in the context of the value they can bring to others. Therefore, their name comes up in parties, jokes, controversy, anything except what they do in business.

Their personal brand is irrelevant to the business they are promoting, because there is no direct connection between their specialty and the brand they are representing to the outside world. For all people know, they could be plumbers, gym instructors, franchise business advisors, or maybe someone not even in business at all.

One reason for this irrelevancy is that they become aware of how important it is to consistently promote a brand tied to their person, but for some reason, they feel like promoting their business specialty alongside their person is somehow distasteful or morally wrong. This is most likely where the expression "shameless self-promotion" was born from. They begin thinking that being honest and sincere means that you should *never* mention your business, nor anything that might reward you financially. Therefore, they build a public image, but remove any connection to their business from it.

> "Every time you communicate with others, you are promoting yourself in some manner or another."

Let me make this clear: Every time you communicate with others, you are promoting yourself in some manner or another. Through what you say, what you share, and the way you do it, you promote your views on issues, your reality, your values, your solutions, and your worldview. It is simply impossible to express yourself without promoting something in the grand marketplace of ideas. You are *always* selling.

If it's true that you are always selling, *then* feeling shame about promoting yourself just shows lack of confidence in your trade. You can either improve the quality of what you offer, or switch towards promoting something else you can be confident about, but you certainly grant no favors to anyone by putting yourself out there with shame about the value that you offer others.

Another cause for people failing to establish relevancy between their personal brand and their business value is that they just haven't been able to find the connection between the two. They might think something like "Well, I'm *authentically* a very fun and dynamic person, but I'm just a boring accountant dealing with numbers and forms. What could one possibly have to do with the other?" The two ideas just seem so distant from each other.

This is a typical example of not seeing the forest through the trees. Business owners and professionals are often so close to their day to day dealings that at times, it all seems like mere drudgery, but this doesn't have to be the case. There are plenty of ways for accountants to inject more fun and dynamism into what they do, and the same is true for every other type of professional. You can begin with your client communication style, your marketing materials, and many other aspects we'll discuss throughout this book.

For example, at my firm YMMY Marketing, we have a particular framework for launching campaigns, which simplifies a very nerve-wracking and critical effort on the part of businesses. A launch can be a do-or-die proposition for many new products. In spite of this, instead of representing our framework with boring diagrams and blueprints, we built an infographic based on the concept of baking an apple pie. The Awareness phase shows a basket of freshly picked apples. The Expectation phase shows the pie baking in the oven, and so on. We infused our love of food and our fun and fresh way to view concepts and ideas into helping our clients become clear about our recommended process for launching their products, brands, and ideas.

The exact same outcome can be achieved through your personal brand. In fact, making sure *you* are present in your business' day to day dealings is what will set you apart from numerous others who perform similar services as you do.

IRRELEVANT VS. ALIGNED

A personal brand that shows full alignment between the expectation someone puts forth and the value they bring to others is on the opposite end of the spectrum from an irrelevant brand. Did you think that the opposite of irrelevant was "relevant"? Well, in this context, relevant would have been too vague. Relevant for what, or for whom? Many people's brands are relevant *to them*, and yet, they're irrelevant to people who may wish to do business with them.

An aligned brand solves the issue of others not taking note of the value you can offer, because it makes you aware and keeps you taking action on your brand efforts. It also ensures that your brand leaves a long-lasting effect on people, so that you can be remembered when it matters the most.

Professionals experience an aligned brand when others refer business to them, even if they might not have asked them to. The fact that they feel a need and that a specific person's name comes to mind means that something is working.

My friend Laura Felix at UBrand has achieved this level of alignment. Whenever we have a question about anything related to printing services, no matter what the challenge is, Laura immediately comes to mind. She has not only established herself as an expert in all matters related to print, but also embodies the personal qualities you hope from a person assisting you towards getting the job done in a timely, cost-efficient manner.

People who have an aligned personal brand are often criticized for "selling out." Others complain that they only talk about business, instead of "just being a human being." First of all, this critique can be valid in cases where a person shoves their business card in people's noses without them asking for it, or tries to whip up a sales appointment from anyone who passes by them. These people are looking to monetize all of their relationships, which is not a good approach in the long term.

It's unfortunate that this situation occurs, but it's not at all what I'm referring to when recommending an aligned personal brand. People who push their business in your face are certainly acting out of desperation. Whereas, an aligned person shows up based on conviction and authority. People think about them when a business need arises precisely because they are **not** pushing their goods upon people, but rather, have led others to come to the realization that they are specialists in their field.

Make no mistake, the person with the aligned personal brand has certainly *influenced* this opinion in people's minds. It rarely happens on its own. Going along and doing what you do every day can only take you so far towards impressing a memorable conviction that you are the right person to talk to.

In Chapter 8, I reveal tactics on how to influence this opinion about you.

Here are some questions to consider around your brand's Alignment:

- Are the ideas and values you stand for in harmony with your mission in business?

- Do the actions you take help others towards a more informed decision when doing business?

- Are you giving people opportunities to ask whether they are interested in what you can offer?

- Are people clear on what to do when they see a need that your business satisfies?

Fourth Challenge: Unremarkable

A person's brand could be visible for the right reasons, true to who that person is, and in alignment with their value in business; yet, one last problem we'll discuss here may affect their potential to leverage their brand for business: being unremarkable. What I mean by this is that the quality of the elements that represent their brand is so poor that people are not motivated to respect them enough to want to do business with them. Even though people might have knowledge of them, very few seem motivated to select them from the multitude of other options available.

In a free market we look to make the best transaction for the most affordable price. Given three options for the same price and with a similar number of features, we will undoubtedly select the one with the highest quality. Even though there might be measurable standards of quality, we also use our subjective opinion to judge quality every now and then.

Therefore, we very often judge quality based on our impression of things. This is why being unremarkable is such a big problem. During the Transaction of Attention, you risk sending forth an expectation that the service you perform and the result others will receive will be of a low quality. This may or may not be true, but you can't place the blame on people for thinking this way in the face of an unremarkable brand.

Another reason an unremarkable brand doesn't help is that, particularly in higher-ticket consultative services, nobody wants to work with a run-of-the-mill service provider. People who hire services want to feel like they're working with someone special, not just one out of a bunch, picked randomly from the crowd.

> "Nobody wants to work with a run-of-the-mill service provider."

Unfortunately, an unremarkable brand sends exactly that impression. It gives the idea that there is nothing admirable or special about this professional. The assets and actions that support their personal brand are of the lowest quality around, so it makes others think that they must not care about standing out. Worse yet, it makes them think that there is nothing they *can* stand out about, because had there been something that separated them from the multitude, they would have made it known to others.

Being unremarkable is pretty much the default state of things for someone who has not given any care to their personal brand. They just get busy in their business and let things be. The best way to ensure that you show up in the exact same way as everyone else in your field is to do exactly this. If you ignore the Transaction of Attention, and you don't take action on anything you read about in this book, then I can predict with absolute certainty that you will blend in among the blur of your competitors.

Aside from inactivity and following the status quo, even when people do take action, they can still cause their brand to be unremarkable. One way they do this is by investing in their personal brand, but select the cheapest tools and resources they can find. Unfortunately, this tends to backfire because they end up putting forth brand assets that they quickly become ashamed about.

Just recently, a company's leader was in the process of publishing their book, so they hired us to design their book cover. Due to their rush to get things done, they decided to hire a cheap freelancer to build a website for their book. As a result, their book cover looks absolutely amazing, but their book website ended up looking awful. You may think I'm joking, but the site doesn't even use one single color in harmony with their book cover!

This lack of attention to their image causes visitors to hesitate, instead of purchasing the book right away. When they arrive at the site, they undoubtedly wonder, "Is the quality of content in this book at the level of the cover, or the level of the website?" Because they are left without a clear picture of the quality they will receive, they hesitate to take any action at all.

People are savvy enough to notice when something is of a lesser level of quality. We are constantly exposed to the highest examples of excellence and creativity, right from our phones, before we even get out of bed and brush our teeth. How is it possible that people think they can dupe others with a brand that displays absolutely nothing worth talking about?

UNREMARKABLE VS. AWESOME

The word "awesome" has lost quite a bit of its meaning through colloquial use. We use it to mean merely the same thing as "okay" or "good." The original meaning of the word indicates something that deserves awe and admiration.

An awesome personal brand is the opposite of an unremarkable one because it stands out as a truly special option in the midst of many other available choices. It shows that the service provided by this person deserves the highest expectation, and often, for this very same reason, people with awesome personal brands charge the highest rates in their industry.

After all, if someone appears to provide the same level of services as everyone else, why would you feel compelled to pay them above the average rate?

One way that I leverage this trait is through the quality of the proposals I send in response to an inquiry. Although other people in my field might send a bland black & white proposal using the default styles in Microsoft Word, my proposals look like they could be published in a magazine. The difference lies in the attention to font styles for titles, subtitles, and format, high-resolution photography, and many other details that sometimes get overlooked by other companies. This is how we close at least 8 out of every 10 proposals we send.

Another example of this quality in excellence involves the explainer videos I produce for my products. Whereas, most people will just go along with one of those cheesy markerboard videos they can get on Fiverr, we will gladly spend a week or two developing an awesome video that will leave people with a lasting impression that our product is of a superior quality.

Your personal brand is not just a pretty logo nor is it your website; it's every second of the experience you give your clients including your boring "day to day" documents. Anything your future clients come into contact with needs to adhere to this standard of awesomeness, which without words, expresses a whole lot about what you stand for.

A few questions to consider around your brand's awesomeness:

- Are you just one out of many others in your field, or can I see from a distance that you stand out from the rest?

- What makes you special above other players in your industry?

- Can people tell from far away, before ever engaging with you, that you offer a superior service over other competitors?

What Does Your Report Card Look Like?

So far, we've talked about four qualities of strong personal brands, all beginning with "A" to make them easier to remember:

- Authentic
- Attractive
- Aligned
- Awesome

Most professionals may embody none of them, or just might have stumbled into one of them. Achieving three of these qualities is great, but a strong personal brand should really have all four of these in place at all times.

The reason all four are required is because lacking in one of them can completely affect any progress or advantage gained from having the others.

For example, someone's brand could be attractive, aligned, and awesome in every respect, but its lack of authenticity turns people off. This is because as we've seen, people wish to be surrounded and do business with people in touch with their real values and personalities.

Another example takes place when a person's brand is attractive, authentic, and awesome, but there is unfortunately no alignment with their business value, and therefore, fails to place them into contact with people who would want to do business with them.

Before you begin applying the tactics found in this book, take 5 minutes to run a quick and honest assessment of your personal brand as it stands today. When answering, be completely honest and truthful to yourself. The more honest you are, the better you will be able to apply the tips you'll find next.

Now go to http://cstps.co/personalbrandreport and follow the quiz you'll find there. With your results in hand, come back here and enjoy the rest of this book.

Beginning with the next chapter, we'll jump into the first element of a solid personal brand, which is all about being Authentic.

CHAPTER 6

Authenticity: Let's Get Real

*Business is closed
only after trust is established.*

All-In On Authenticity

So far, we've talked about the need to differentiate yourself and stand out among other professionals who are in the same business as you. It is really the only way to excel at what you do, because the alternative is to be just like everyone else. According to the law of supply and demand, if something is in high supply, there will be less demand for it. This is precisely because there is so much of it available.

The way to beat the quicksand of high supply is to highlight yourself where you offer a completely different experience. Many people struggle with this because it's hard to imagine how in the world they can become different from everyone else who does what they do. They scratch their heads and wonder how to go about this because in their deepest thoughts, they know that they are just one more player, and as such, are replaceable at any moment.

> "There are many of them — competing professionals in your field — yet, only one of you."

The death of differentiation occurs precisely when you begin to see yourself as a swappable professional, but here's the key: there are many of them — competing professionals in your field — yet, only one of *you*. This is the most liberating thought in our goal to rise above the masses, and if you don't see the power of thinking this way, I will kindly invite you to read this statement once again:

There is only one of *you*.

The difficulty in differentiating yourself and standing out comes as a result of looking away from this fact. Maybe we were taught that we shouldn't boast, or that paying too much attention to oneself was a selfish, egomaniacal thing to do.

Let met be completely honest and say that developing your personal brand and pitching it confidently *can* become an exercise in puffing up your ego. It can drain every drop of compassion and empathy from you, and can fool you into thinking that you are the best in the world and that nobody else matters. It *can* perform all sorts of evil tricks on your mind and your ego…but it doesn't have to.

Aspiring to become the CEO of a company can be an exercise to puff your ego, but it can also be the most efficient way to implement your leadership skills and to serve customers by providing them with a valuable product at a reasonable price. Aspiring to become the coach of a sports team can be an effort to fill yourself with foolish pride, or it can be a means to put your coaching skills to good use and help the team reach the gold.

The thread that ties these examples and our subject at hand is leadership. Open your eyes and realize that you are the executive leader of the Brand of You. Whether you use this platform for evil just to boast, or you use your talents to make a difference in this world is entirely up to you.

The means don't change your true intention, and if your intention is to be an egomaniac, you'll surely find easier ways to puff yourself up than what I recommend in this book. Dig deeply inside yourself before walking down this path. Why is it that you've agreed that the Brand of You is precisely what will help you stand out and support your business?

Only One Of You

T he key to becoming more authentic and unique is to forge the Brand of You around who you *really* are.

If it's true that there's only one of you, then you need to make sure that your brand reflects who you are as a person as closely as possible.

Some people might get a bit nervous when reading this. They think that their business is a bit stuffy and boring, and that people asking about their products and services don't really want to deal with their casual and real selves, but rather, with folks who are all buttoned-up and "professional". This couldn't be further from the truth. People actually do want to deal with authentic people.

They want to connect with others who are happy to offer their advice blended in with their most intimate life situations and raw experiences. They want to deal with people whom they can understand and identify with, and who can accept them. What they absolutely don't want to deal with is stuffy and pretentious salesmen, but this is unfortunately the majority of whom they come into contact with.

Before I realized that this was the key to becoming more authentic, I used to think I was supposed to mimic how the most successful people in my space spoke, wrote, and behaved. I thought, "Well, people already like this guy, so let me just try to be more like him." Well, that experiment totally failed, because the fact of the matter is that people didn't like that guy because of the things he did, but because that guy was being 100% authentic around who he was.

People admire seeing someone confident about who they are, because it shows that they are in tune with their true self, and their insecurities and fears have not been able to stand in the way of their desire to serve other people. Everyone secretly admires this level of confidence, so most people sway towards those who have already reached it.

Although there are a ton of self-development lessons to be learned here, I'm not really telling you this to help you become more confident in life. Although, if you do achieve this as a secondary effect, a bit more confidence certainly wouldn't be a bad thing! I want you to discover how to highlight yourself among a crowd of others who may or may not perform as well as you do. Step out and express who you truly are. You will be surprised at how easily people will connect with you.

Clarify and Stand Out

Developing the Brand of You is the best way to clarify your unique value amidst a multitude of options. Whether you're looking to drive more consultation opportunities, more sales conversations, or just more valuable business connections of any kind, your goal will be to increase the number of *relationships* you engage in. Human beings seek value, and are looking to receive this value through relationships with other humans.

Relationships are based on expectations. When you meet with a stranger, you have certain expectations of what should take place before you decide to engage further with him or her. But when you visit a friend, you already have an idea of who your friend is and the values they stand for. You've created an expectation through many past interactions in which you've come to learn about who they are. So, the idea of this particular friend is very clear in your mind.

One of the most effective ways to create expectations in people's minds is through developing your brand. Quite simply, it takes showing up consistently based on the same aspects, personality, and stories you identified as true to your own self.

Corporations work hard on documenting every specific guideline about their brand to ensure that no new expression contradicts anything previously agreed upon. They do this because if they don't, they face a situation in which they break consistency and confuse their audience. The Brand of You is no different. It requires prep-work, lots of it. It also requires that you refer back to your guidelines to make sure that you're building up, instead of starting from scratch each time.

In this chapter, you will discover the qualities of your authentic brand so that you are absolutely clear on how to express who you are and who you are not.

In the following exercise, you already have a huge advantage that even corporate teams for the world's largest brands will never have: the source of your brand's prime matter. This prime matter is inside of you, and you've been carrying it with you every second, every hour, and every day of every year you've been alive. When in doubt — and you *will* have doubt every once in a while — the essential brand book that will cause you to be unique is with you wherever you go.

I'm not asking you to become anyone else in order to work on the Brand of You. I'm inviting you to do exactly the opposite. Be your unique self and build your unique brand. This is your chance to stand out, embrace it!

An OCEAN Of Distinction

One way to keep yourself grounded in who you are is to begin by discovering what you already have to work with. You could do a little bit of guesswork around your personality, but there is no reason to do so given so many great resources to help you know yourself more deeply.

The University of Cambridge developed a fascinating model for behavioral psychology that studies five traits of human beings, and illustrates how they tend to behave in certain situations. The model is called the Five-Factor Model, and is also known as the OCEAN model due to the initials of each of the five traits.

As you read this list, give yourself a score from 1 to 5 stars — 1 being a trait you don't identify much with, and 5 one that you believe you are very strong in — for each of the traits in this OCEAN model:

Openness: Curiosity, preference towards variety and new experiences. An inclination towards a variety of activities instead of a strict routine.

☆ ☆ ☆ ☆ ☆

Conscientiousness: A tendency to plan things ahead, to favor self-discipline and reliability rather than spontaneity in behavior.

☆ ☆ ☆ ☆ ☆

Extraversion: Sociability and a drive towards seeking stimulation in the company of others.

☆ ☆ ☆ ☆ ☆

Agreeableness: A strong pull towards being compassionate and cooperative.

☆ ☆ ☆ ☆ ☆

Neuroticism: A tendency to experience negative emotions very easily, such as anger, anxiety, and depression.

☆ ☆ ☆ ☆ ☆

You can also spend 15-minutes on http://cstps.co/personalitytest and perform the test there. Once you complete it, it will present you with an accurate assessment of your personality based on how you scored in each of these traits.

What do the results say about you? The goal is to discover what I like to call your "factory settings."

When you buy a new computer, it comes from the factory with a few standard settings that are pretty much set across other similar computers coming from the same factory. It's what makes each computer reliable and functional. From there, we all tweak, modify, and extend our computers to our liking, until each one takes on a life of its own. This is why some of us feel like our computers have their own personality after we've owned them for some time.

This OCEAN model can help reveal some pretty strong tendencies toward being a certain way, which you were already born with. Here's what your score reveals about the stuff you're made of:

- **Openness:** A person with a high score in this category indicates a general appreciation for new experiences such as art, emotion, adventures, and curiosities. A person with a low score in this category might show traits of a person beholden to tradition, consistency, and persevering in their ways.

- **Conscientiousness:** A person with a high score in this category shows a tendency to be organized, dependable, and show self-discipline. A person with a low score in this category may appear as sloppy, disorganized, and at times, reckless.

- **Extraversion:** A person with a high score in this category shows a person that is most satisfied when surrounded by other people. A person with a low score in this category shows a person who would rather be solitary, avoids crowds, and is a bit more reserved.

- **Agreeableness:** A person with a high score in this category shows a tendency to be cooperative, amicable, and compassionate, but can often be perceived as submissive. A person with a low score in this category tends to be someone who is argumentative, conflicted, and loves debating others.

- **Neuroticism:** A person with a high score in this category reveals someone who is easily given to negative emotions such as anger, anxiety, and irritability. A person with a low score in this category indicates someone who is stable, centered, and in control.

After uncovering your "factory settings," you'll notice that it really is a misuse of your time and your focus to try to change them. There are no wrong answers here. You can build an authentic Brand of You from wherever you land.

Your Influential Persona

Now that you're a bit more in touch with your default traits, it's time for us to work on bringing your unique essence into the world. Developing your Influential Persona will be a key exercise to create a bridge between who you really are and how you want to be perceived in a business environment.

What is a Persona? In ancient Greece and Rome, a "persona" was a mask used by actors in theatrical performances. In these theatrical performances, there was no theater lighting, microphones, sound systems, or any of the devices we use today to ensure that members of the audience can understand what is happening on stage. Aside from their masks, there wasn't much else to help them carry the message they were trying to convey clearly from the stage to the seats.

If the actors didn't wear their personas, the people sitting in the stands would just see figures flapping their arms and moving side to side. It would have been extremely difficult to point out who the bad guy was, who the good guy was, who was sad, who was angry, etc. The main function of the persona was not at all to *hide* the actor's character, but rather the exact opposite. It was meant to *amplify* their character so that it was easier to discern by those at a perceptive disadvantage.

A similar disadvantage takes place when you are in a crowded space in your industry, and with attention being such a scarce resource as it is today, your persona can easily get lost in the crowd if it's not clear enough. With so many professionals doing the same thing you do, and acting in the exact same manner, everyone seems to be so similar when looking from the outside. Therefore, it becomes difficult to take notice of what makes you different.

I can't tell you how many networking meetings I've gone to where I've bumped into groups of people in the same industry, such as financial planners or insurance agents. You talk to one, and it feels like you've talked to all of them. They have the exact same pitch, the exact same personality, and the exact same approach. I don't mean to disrespect financial planners nor people in insurance, but seriously! You could close your eyes and swat your hands in the air at a networking meeting and you'll hit at least five of them who talk and act and walk the same exact way. But if we're honest, this situation holds true in most professions I can think of. Even in mine!

A persona will help you amplify who you are authentically and what you are made of, so that others can tell you apart from the masses.

Your Influential Persona is primarily built out of three components: your Aspects, your Personality, and your Story. Let's look at each component in detail to discover how your persona should appear in order to represent who you are in the most accurate, *authentic* manner.

Your Influential Aspects

T he first element we'll discuss about your influential persona involves the building blocks of what makes you...well, you. One way to keep your brand 100% grounded in authenticity is to always pull from the source. That is, pull from who you truly are. It is what makes you unique and different from everyone else, and therefore, it's your best insurance against coming out with a synthetic brand that will disappoint others.

Just like the five OCEAN traits we just looked at, your Aspects are not changeable and at this point, it's too late to modify them. This is actually a good thing, because our goal is for our brand to be as raw, real, and truthful as possible. By uncovering our real Aspects, we wipe out any possibility of manipulating the source of our brand.

There are many advantages around discovering your Aspects, but here are just a few:

1. **They help you become more confident.** Once you know that your Aspects are what they are, and that they are precisely what makes you unique, you'll be less nervous about expressing your true self when pitching your business.

2. **They help you remain authentic.** Many people try to develop their brand by looking up to other people who are more successful

than they are and emulating them, but pulling from your Aspects forces you to look inward, to discover your own unique strengths.

3. **They make everything else about developing your brand a lot easier.** Because you're not starting with something obscure or hidden from sight, you're gaining insight from what you've known about yourself all along.

As you can see, it is highly beneficial to take a moment to define these. Later on I will challenge you to speak about your industry topic from your unique voice. Your Aspects help define four different vantage points, which in combination make your perspective difficult to replicate.

Your Aspects are comprised of these four main elements:

- **Your Origin:** Where you came from, and how you began doing what you do. This is particularly important, because it's rare to see two professionals in any field with the exact same origin. Even siblings who grew up together will remember different events as their most formative ones.

- **Your Abilities:** Your advantages in what you do. Here, we're looking to define what you do particularly well, whether it's directly advantageous to your professional career or indirectly so.

- **Your Flaws:** The tasks or situations you are challenged by. It's great to place your finger on things you don't do particularly well, so that you can work on them, but also use them to demonstrate your humanity. One of the key methods to demonstrating authenticity is to not be afraid to show that you are aware of your challenges and your weaknesses.

- **Your Polar Opposite:** A description of a person that stands for everything you are not. Usually, your polar opposite will be a type of person that you want to differentiate yourself from in everything you do. It doesn't mean that you are not surrounded by this type of person right now, only that you would like to make very clear that you're not like them.

One of the clearest templates of personal brand Aspects is found in comic book characters. Classic comic book characters are the ultimate example of consistency and clarity in the brand they represent. As an example, think about Spider-Man. As soon as you read his name, the iconic blue and red suit with webbing lines all over come right into your mind. When you think about Spider-Man's *character*, you can also pick up his Aspects almost immediately.

- **Origin:** Grew up in New York as a dorky kid, bitten by a radioactive spider.

- **Abilities:** Sticks to walls, slings web, super-strength, etc.

- **Flaws:** Sabotages his abilities through insecurity and emotional bursts.

- **Polar Opposite:** Chaotic power (like Doctor Octopus)

Now, you might be thinking, "This is ridiculous. I'm not a comic book character." Of course you're not. You're interested in how this advice applies to developing your business, so let's look at whether we can discern the aspects of a recognized figure in the business scene.

Let's examine Daymond John, the successful entrepreneur and one of the sharks on the hit TV show "Shark Tank." Has he defined his Aspects? I think that if you spend any amount of time listening to him or reading his books, you can see that he very consistently pulls from his source:

- **Origin:** Grew up in Queens, NY. Attended school every other week, as he also had to work from a very young age.

- **Abilities:** Compassionate and down-to-earth. Loves motivating the little guy.

- **Flaws:** Dyslexic. Can sometimes be too transparent with his emotions.

- **Polar Opposite:** People begging for favors and people who disregard form over function.

You can see that without these clearly defined Aspects, there would be no Daymond John as we know him. If it were possible to go back in time and change just one of these, his personal brand would turn out to be completely different to that which we have come to know.

Now, I'd like to invite you to think about yourself. What are *your* Aspects? Here are some questions to help you discover them:

Origin. What was the most formative experience you lived through, whether to shape your character, or to get you started in the industry you now work in? What is unique about your upbringing?

Abilities. What can you do particularly well? What can you produce in a rather effortless manner? If you were put on the spot, what topic could you speak about without making a mistake?

Flaws. Which situations or tasks are particularly challenging for you? What are some things that don't come out the way they should when you attempt them?

Polar Opposite. Which type of people do you feel are the absolute opposite of who you are? Which type of personality are you constantly clarifying that you are distinctly different from?

Once you can see your Aspects clearly, you'll begin to discover ways to express them through the way you sell yourself, and the tone you use.

Your Influential Personality

In this next component of your Influential Persona, we'll look to define your attitude and style when expressing your values to the world. People who develop their personal brand stand out from the rest of the professionals in their field because somehow they've managed to communicate in a distinctive manner, even though the core ideas they're communicating may be similar to others. It's not about *what* they say, but rather *how* they say it.

Their message may not change in essence, but it changes in form based on the personality that they've taken on for their Influential Persona.

Imagine someone who is trying to establish their brand, yet one day they show up as bold and critical, and another day they are soft-spoken and timid. They wouldn't create an impression on others because their personality doesn't stay on track.

Instead of defining their personality, they shift with the way they are feeling each day of the week. The problem with this approach is that we all wake up feeling differently from one day to the next, but this doesn't mean that we should anchor our outward personality based on our changing emotional state.

A much better approach is to define a personality that "fits" who we are and what we're trying to achieve, and stick to it no matter how we wake up. Just because we aren't portraying exactly how we feel a certain day, it doesn't mean that we are now being fake. On the contrary, we'll be defining our personality ahead of time on the essence of who we are, not on our changing state of how we feel that particular day.

In the following pages, I will give you a tour along six different personality archetypes that work towards influencing others by setting clear expectations of who you are. You might think that you're too unique and one-of-a-kind for one of these to fit you perfectly, but please don't resist against these personality archetypes. They have worked for thousands of people in business.

When you *don't* have a defined personality for your brand yet, it helps to begin with one of these six, and then develop it further from there.

After each Personality archetype, you'll see five star outlines. Fill in the number of stars depending on how much you feel each archetype fits you. For example, if you think one of them fits you perfectly, fill in all five stars. On the other hand, if you feel another one has nothing to do with you, just keep them empty.

THE RING LEADER

This personality archetype fits perfectly with people who are very direct in their approach towards others, and usually state their ideas very "matter-of-factly."

Ring Leaders are interested in stating things as they are. They are not about seeking a consensus among other people's opinions and their own. For this reason, they are often perceived by others as brash and arrogant. Others follow them because they display strong assertiveness and often take initiative before others do.

It's usually not kosher to communicate with swear words, but some Ring Leaders don't really care. They're all about saying things as they come out, and full transparency — as shocking as it may be — is much more important than political correctness or appearances.

Chances are, if you hated the idea of selecting a personality archetype back when I described this exercise, you might be a Ring Leader.

An example of a Ring Leader is Richard Branson, the successful founder of the Virgin Group. Whenever he makes his appearances or communicates to the public in some manner, he is extremely direct in how he expresses his ideas and core beliefs, and nothing in what he says, gives you any inkling that he is willing to negotiate.

As I write this book, the President of the United States is Donald J. Trump, another Ring Leader. No matter what you think of him as a politician, you know that he will tell you exactly what is on his mind. He even tweets in a very Ring Leader fashion, predictably ending any critical statements with the one word: "Sad!"

How much of a Ring Leader are you?

☆ ☆ ☆ ☆ ☆

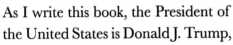

THE NEWS REPORTER

This personality is all about being informed about the latest and greatest in their industry, and openly informing others about what they have found out. News Reporters' biggest frustration occurs when someone delivers breaking news before they get a chance to.

This is why News Reporter personalities are the biggest victims of FOMO (Fear Of Missing Out). They are so worried they'll miss something, so they try to be plugged into some reliable news source at all times in order to be in the know. Often times, news about their industry gets mixed up with pop culture news and random information, because at the end of the day, news is news, no matter what it's about.

Many times, the News Reporter will drop tidbits of info they've picked up as part of any ordinary conversation, even if the main topic isn't even related to the latest news. The reason they do this is because establishing the fact that they are up to speed in the latest and greatest *is* a main topic in any conversation. Therefore, snippets recently read in newspapers, magazines, or books, info picked up while driving and listening to radio or a podcast, all help color the conversations and establish who the real news authority is.

Perez Hilton, the celebrity gossiper — not to be confused with *Paris* Hilton — is an example of a News Reporter personality. I would fail even the easiest test on the life of the Kardashians, but if you want someone to bring you up to speed on this famous family, all you need to do is ask Perez Hilton.

The interesting thing is that a News Reporter doesn't have to talk exclusively about gossip nor celebrities. Robert Scoble, a pundit about all things tech, is an excellent example of a News Reporter. He spends time patiently listening to people on the front lines of his industry (particularly related to technology) and is hyper-sensitive about new developments arising. He influences a huge audience, and those who know him, know that Scoble represents a down-to-earth, non-exaggerated approach to technology.

How much of a News Reporter are you?

THE LAB RAT

A personality that is in constant experimentation mode on themselves is what I call a Lab Rat. These are the people who use themselves as test subjects because they feel that people who live through certain experiences are the most well-equipped to talk about them. They even feel icky if someone ever asks their opinion about a topic they haven't personally experimented with yet.

The Lab Rat's life is all about taking glances at their checklist of things they haven't yet done, and placing them in their to-do list to get them done in the near future.

The payoff for a Lab Rat is much more than just the first-hand experience. It also has to do with the authority they feel they are able to establish when speaking to others. Some people know about a topic because they've merely studied it, but Lab Rats feel like they *really know* what they're talking about. Placing themselves in harm's way or spending their own hard-earned money is the ultimate badge of honor and authenticity for a Lab Rat.

Tim Ferris, the best-selling author of the Four-Hour Workweek is a great example of a Lab Rat. Whether it's through fitness, supplementation, or even methods to learn a new language, Tim strives to speak from his own experiences way more often than quoting an authority on a subject. Not that he puts anyone who has studied a topic down, but he will spend much more time talking about what he personally found while living through his own experiment.

The .NET software programming community knows Scott Hanselman for a similar reason. When he talks about a subject, he not only does so from his vast knowledge, but also publishes about his experiments developing software for others to see. He is rarely ever seen discussing a topic that he hasn't first spent countless hours working on.

How much of a Lab Rat are you?

THE HUMBLE HERO

A Humble Hero personality is one that is fully invested in helping others. Don't let the word "Humble" fool you, though. Although they're certainly not bent on blatantly yammering to the world about why they're so cool, they are well aware that what they do for others is absolutely amazing. They just let others discover it for themselves.

The Humble Hero is in tune with their awesome life-changing and business-changing abilities. They don't need others to affirm them, nor do they expect them to. Their abilities are placed in the service of people around them, and for them, seeing others push forward is enough of a reward.

It's safe to say that the Humble Hero not only feels a duty to serve others, but also derives pleasure by seeing others around them succeed and improve. They often ask reflective questions and listen to other people's responses, but this is their special skill in disguise. This is their ability to make others think deeply and arrive at a greater insight, often while feeling like they arrived there completely on their own.

The Humble Hero has the ability to say what everyone already has on their mind, at the right moment and with the right words. Their main purpose is to make *others* feel like the real heroes.

Dale Carnegie, the incredibly famous author of *How To Win Friends and Influence People*, was a prime example of a Humble Hero. In his books, he generously shares stories and tips, but by doing so, he manages to help you connect the dots in your own mind as you read. When you read his work, you come out feeling empowered and feeling like you can get the job done.

Another example of a Humble Hero is Chris Brogan, the best-selling author and speaker (who also wrote the foreword for my first book *Digital BACON*...thanks again, Chris!) has gathered a large community of entrepreneurs focused on building themselves and their businesses, and Chris does such a great job at helping every member of his community feel like they can absolutely do this. I am personally grateful to him for inspiring me and showing me an example of how a Humble Hero should act.

How much of a Humble Hero are you?

THE JOKESTER

"LOL!" is this personality's favorite reaction, because The Jokester lives to make fun of themselves and cause other people to laugh. Telling a joke that completely flops is the biggest disappointment for them. The Jokester's insurance policy against this tragedy is to cross the line farther than most people would be comfortable with.

With regard to topics about themselves which can bring out a chuckle in others, The Jokester has absolutely zero sacred cows. You can laugh at their appearance, their cultural background, their family, their pets, or anything else about them. Anything goes because no matter what you're laughing at, they've already been laughing at themselves first.

They are often quite irreverent around sensitive topics, such as politics or religion. This causes some overly sensitive people to be turned off, but most people recognize that whatever they said is coming from a Jokester.

They are more willing to give them a free pass even if the joke might seem offensive on the surface. If The Jokester is capable of making fun of his own mother, what wouldn't he make fun of?

And yet, people enjoy Jokesters so much that even if they make fun of everything, in the rare occasions they do speak seriously, people are somehow able to recognize the shift and tend to pay proper attention to them. Although their standard M.O. is to incessantly come up with jokes, their credibility isn't affected one bit when the situation merits it.

Conan O'Brien has built a personality that is a pure, unfiltered Jokester. He is the first person willing to place himself in the most incredibly ridiculous and embarrassing circumstances. Therefore, he gets a license to speak about things that most of us could never even begin to discuss, because we'd be afraid of offending nine-tenths of the population.

Jon Acuff is also an example of a Jokester. He became famous for his blog, *Stuff Christians Do*, where he made fun of quirky habits found in churches across America. He has continued his style of making fun of things millions of people consider sacred, but in reality, he can also be found as a keynote speaker at large Christian conferences, preaching and encouraging others. His jokes haven't eroded his ability to make people listen to him. On the contrary, they've just opened doors for him. People are brought in because of the jokes, and stay because of his wholesome, impactful ideas.

How much of a Jokester are you?

CAPTAIN CONTRARIAN

The last of the personality archetypes we'll go over is one you can always find rallying against an idea or group of people they oppose. In the previous section about Aspects, we talked about identifying your Polar Opposite. Well, Captain Contrarian makes a living off of being engaged in constant battle against their Polar Opposite.

In fact, Captain Contrarians are known more for the things they are fighting against than for their own stances on topics. Whether through sarcasm or serious debate, you can rely on them to find out what is wrong about a certain ideology or attitude.

This personality often comes across as combative and defensive, but they don't mind because this is exactly the way they seek to come across. They are happy to annoy and ridicule those who represent their Polar Opposite. Ironically, those people in the group they're fighting against often help make Captain Contrarians popular, simply by attempting to defend themselves. Most of the time,

they speak negatively about the Captain, but as they say, "Any press is good press."

Criticism is one of Captain Contrarian's favorite forms of content and pointing their finger at others is perfectly normal. If anyone is going to show why "the other side" is wrong, it might as well be them. Moreover, it *better* be them first, because an opportunity to criticize their arch-enemies can never be squandered.

Milo Yiannopoulos, the former Senior Editor for controversial alt-right news and commentary site Breitbart, is a prime example of a Captain Contrarian. He is loudly vocal against feminism, liberals, the social justice movement, and many other groups he disagrees with. Milo supposedly stands for an alternative view of the world, but what that alternative actually stands for often gets lost in the midst of his hard criticism of those other positions.

Rachel Maddow, the political anchor famous for her appearances on MSNBC, is an example of a Captain Contrarian on the opposite side of the political spectrum from Milo. Rachel is a vocal critic of anything even an inch towards the right of center. She is known for her hard words and long diatribes against the U.S. Republican/Conservative factions, directed towards both their key politicians as well as their policies.

Although Captain Contrarians can be more easily identified in the political battlefield, they can also be found in business. For example, renowned American investor Warren Buffett is unabashedly vocal about his opposition to stances and actions commonly taken by stock traders including high-frequency trading, buying "hot stocks," and even living a lavish lifestyle.

How much of a Captain Contrarian are you?

After reading these descriptions and filling in the stars based on how much you identify with each personality, you should now have an idea of which personality archetype best reflects who you are and how you wish to be portrayed.

Your Influential Story

U p to this point, we've defined how to bring out who you are in a manner that is concrete and memorable. Yet, one element that is often forgotten when developing our personal brand is our story.

Let's face it. Human beings are story junkies. From etchings on cave walls, through millions of myths in all sizes and levels of complexity, to binge-watching multiple seasons of a show in a day or two, we rise and fall on the strength of the stories we consume, but also on the ones we tell others.

If you haven't dedicated serious effort into defining your Influential Persona within a storytelling framework, you run the risk of your brand appearing stale and static. Stories, by definition, can only be dynamic. It's okay for product brands to remain static for long periods of time, but when it comes to personal brands, there will always be back stories involved, and stories develop through time.

Stories do not only help catch people's attention, but they also keep them engaged. Our stories will always have a "To Be Continued" essence. In other words, we'll define our story up to the present point, but what keeps people engaged is that our story will continue developing. When people understand where you're coming from, it'll be much easier to lock their minds on how you continue developing from here.

Defining your influential story doesn't mean that you will be telling it every time you speak or when you communicate with others. What it does mean is that when you tell others about where you're at and where you're heading towards, you are doing so *from* the basis of your influential story. In other words, you are aware that any new stories are just a continuation of your foundational story framework.

Allow me to use myself as an example. One of the foundational elements of my story is that my father was a military exile, being forced to exit his homeland of the Dominican Republic due to very dangerous conditions shortly after a hard-fought revolution in 1965. He traveled to the United States, where he worked very strenuously to establish himself within a completely different culture and society. Some of my dearest memories as a child in New York City are of my father teaching other hard-working men about how to repair electric appliances. He would take me to his classroom every other week. He would also hold meetings with members of the Dominican community in New York, to motivate them to take democratic action. Through his example, my father taught me the value of helping and supporting others, no matter if you came from difficult circumstances.

When I was much older, I discovered something amazing. While studying the origin of the name my parents gave me "Alexander," I discovered that the original Greek form *Aleks-andros* means "Helper of men [humans]." Since then, I've accepted that my life's purpose on this planet is to help other people. Quite surprisingly, this purpose is in congruence with the example my father gave me.

Now, when I present a client with a set of solutions, or when I offer the opportunity to coach others, I do so concretely from the perspective that what I do flows naturally from my life's purpose to employ my abilities and experiences towards supporting others. Even the book you are reading now is a manifestation of my sincere desire to see you succeed. I would even dare to say that, even if you had never heard my story before, it makes complete sense in the context of what you do know about me after reading how I've framed this topic.

Can you see how a story can connect *who you are* with *what you do*, and more importantly, *why* you do what you do?

I'd like to emphasize the previous point about your *why*. Our lives are a wildly complex texture of thousands of different stories, but you need to define the story that reveals *why* you entered into this line of business. Leave aside the obvious reason that it is your way to generate money to support yourself and your family. *Why* did you choose to do this instead of something else? What experience gave you clarity that this field is a better fit for you than anything else you might have chosen?

Another key to this exercise is that stories typically have a beginning, a middle, and an end. Therefore, the end of your story must somehow connect with what you do today. Imagine yourself telling your story in front of a group of people. When you finish telling it, those people listening must walk away feeling that what you do today — to be more direct, your presentation of the products or services that you offer — makes total sense to them.

Throughout the following pages, I share seven different story frameworks. Just like in the previous section, you should score each one from 0 to 5 stars based on how much it helps give your own life story some structure and makes it come alive.

STORY FRAMEWORK 1: FALL AND REDEMPTION

"I once was lost, but then I found _____."

This story framework begins with a meaningful personal or professional challenge, one that others may relate to regardless of whether they have lived through a similar experience or not.

After defining the element that challenged you, outline a key lesson or decision that made a profound difference and helped you overcome that challenge.

The key to this story framework is that the nature of the challenge must be highly difficult and negative. For example, bankruptcy, a severe disease, a dire family situation, very high employee turnover, addictions, and others like these tend to appear commonly in Fall and Redemption stories.

How much does the "Fall and Redemption" story apply to you?

☆ ☆ ☆ ☆ ☆

STORY FRAMEWORK 2: "THE TRANSFORMATION EFFECT"

"I was once _____, but now I'm _____."

This framework is similar to the previous one, but instead of describing an external challenge or experience, this one is about a struggle with your own identity. Here, you are admitting *being* or having been a certain negative way. Your behaviors, attitudes, and habits used to be of an off-putting nature for others and for yourself. Then, something happened that completely transformed the core of who you are.

The Transformation Effect can also be applied to your business situation. Your company's essence could have been of a certain type, but has now become a completely different company. This change may have taken place based on how you've personally transformed your stance toward a particular subject.

In this story framework, the transformation must be *irreversible*. We're not just talking about a simple adjustment or a slight shift in focus. In order for this story to work, a complete reinvention has to have taken place, so what comes out the other end has to be practically unrecognizable from what you began with.

How much does the "Transformation Effect" story apply to you?

☆ ☆ ☆ ☆ ☆

STORY FRAMEWORK 3: US VS. THEM

"I'm now a proud _____, and no longer a silly _____."

This story may be similar to the previous one, as they both deal with an evolution in between contrasting identities. The main difference is that "Us vs. Them" emphasizes the fact that whatever you once were is now your Polar Opposite. This framework exposes your vulnerability in that at one point in time, you actually *were* a member of the group that you now openly expose and point your finger at.

Though it may seem like a hypocritical story on the surface , it's not hypocritical once you delve into it. What you are really doing is admitting that anyone could be duped into being a certain way, just like you were. Now that you've seen the light, you're more than happy to talk about why remaining in that group is nothing but a stupid decision.

This framework doesn't mince words when outlining who a person should and should not be. More than attacking others, your target is that version of you who you cannot identify with any more. Because of the fact that you are openly exposing your vulnerability by admitting to having lived a life that you can no longer tolerate, your story comes across as highly authentic.

How much does the "Us vs. Them" story apply to you?

☆ ☆ ☆ ☆ ☆

STORY FRAMEWORK 4: AMAZING DISCOVERY

"My life completely changed when I discovered _____."

This story framework also sounds similar to the Transformation Effect, but this one doesn't require beginning at a particularly challenging aspect of your life. Your life could have been perfectly normal and average. Yet, you experienced a significant upgrade after coming upon a specific insight or truth that was revealed to you.

In this story framework, the emphasis is placed on the fact or insight discovered and the effect it had on you. It does not focus on the state or condition of things before landing upon the discovery. In other words, describing the fact or truth you discovered is essential, but it is just as important to describe *how* this truth changed your view on who you are and what you do.

The insight you discovered shouldn't be something easy to figure out by anyone, nor should it be a rather obvious fact. If it is, it might make your story come across as disingenuous. This special piece of information should only be discoverable by a few select people, or may even be something that only you could have found.

How much does the "Amazing Discovery" story apply to you?

Story Framework 5: Valuable Secret

"The secret to ___ was right in front of me the whole time."

This story describes a meaningful effort towards figuring something out. It often includes repeated failure to land at the solution, usually resulting in frustration of some kind.

The person stumbles upon the surprising fact that the solution was with them — or within them — all along. Whereas the main character in the Amazing Discovery framework arrives at a particularly hidden insight, the Valuable Secret protagonist finds that the secret wasn't actually hidden at all. They just couldn't see it.

They only needed to realize that what they had overlooked was exactly what they needed this whole time. This framework also emphasizes the secret that is revealed to them, not because it was obscure or hidden, but because it was the last thing they expected it to be.

How much does the "Valuable Secret" story apply to you?

STORY FRAMEWORK 6: LIFELONG PASSION

"Since I was young, I've always been passionate about _____."

In this framework, the protagonist taps into a drive or inclination they realize they've had for their whole life. In stark contrast with some of the previous frameworks, there is no "before and after" here.

The outstanding fact this story is grounded upon is that the main character has remained on track in their true passion for a long period of time. Their faithfulness and dedication to what has driven them validates why they continue doing what they do, and why they're so passionate about it.

The main character in this story is the opposite of a "fly by night" professional. It describes someone who has been on a consistent track, honing their skills for a very long time, possibly since childhood.

This story framework also doesn't require that they be working in the same profession during this period. Often times, this story fits even a person who has just made a career change. In this instance, the Lifelong Passion can help validate why the career change was made and is often a solid reason to abandon one career to take on another that is much more in line with this lifetime devotion.

How much does the "Lifelong Passion" story apply to you?

☆ ☆ ☆ ☆ ☆

STORY FRAMEWORK 7: DISCIPLE TO MASTER

"By applying the truths of___, I've become a master at ___."

This last framework builds the protagonist up as a true master of their trade, one who acquires their abilities and skills by following a very precise process. This process is the emphasis of the story framework we're discussing here.

In other words, it's not so much about how the person is a master — although there must be zero fear about establishing oneself as such —

but the specific philosophy, set of steps, or transformational process must be highlighted as the methodology followed to go from total beginner to elite level.

Having started out as a total beginner can definitely be a main component of this story. This framework begins by describing how helpless and weak the person was before beginning the process. Then it emphasizes how necessary the process towards mastery was. It will then outline the stark contrast between the current master status and what used to be their reality, along with their past struggles, challenges, or limitations.

How much does the "Disciple to Master" story apply to you?

You've just taken a tour through each of the seven story frameworks, and have scored each one based on how well you think each one applies to your own story. You should now one of these frameworks rising above the rest as very closely applicable to you.

In the event you've given the highest score to two or more of them, you might want to go through a tie-breaker round where you decide which of them helps bring your story to life a bit more.

Real vs Realistic

When describing your Influential Persona, it's helpful to understand the distinction between real and realistic. In all honesty, you might have gone through an unbelievable, even miraculous experience in your life, but one that is 100% real in all its details. You might have very rare abilities, which only one in 10,000 people have.

Unfortunately, these facts might be so implausible that instead of astonishing those around you, it causes them to pause in their tracks and hesitate to listen further due to their disbelief. This might strike you as unfair — after all, you *were* being authentic! — yet, people have heard so many gross exaggerations and fake stories of success that it's reasonable to have doubt about anything that sounds similar to these.

Sadly, because people are skeptical about these real facts about you, it fails to produce the result you're looking for: attention. This is why I recommend evaluating whether your story is *realistic*, and not just real. In other words, you need to judge whether your story might sound familiar and relatable to others. If it doesn't, I recommend you tone it down a bit, or leave out details until you engage deeper with them.

For example, when I meet people for the first time, I never tell them that after a hard day, I wind down by playing Bach on the piano, nor that my third language is Japanese, nor that I studied in one of the most distinguished art schools in New York City. Although these are real facts, I know that someone who doesn't know me might think I'm exaggerating to make myself look smarter and more skilled than I really am, and therefore be put off before I got a chance to tell more about myself.

I find that by toning down my story and my abilities to just the details that are realistic, and then letting them discover those other things after we've engaged further, I stand a much better chance of catching their attention and starting a conversation.

Putting It All Together

So far you've gone through your four Aspects, have chosen one among the six Personality archetypes, and have picked one of the seven Story frameworks as the one that fits best around your true story. If you *didn't* define these and are just reading through that's fine, but to be honest just reading along won't be as beneficial for you.

Developing your personal brand isn't something you can just read through quickly and expect to get the outcomes from it. The work you put into this is what will separate you from the hordes of others who never even begin defining these important building blocks of their personal brand.

If you did perform the exercises presented so far, then you will refer back to them as you continue reading this book. I'll be asking you to whip these out at certain key points of the book so that the other elements of your personal brand are grounded in your authentic self.

CHAPTER 7

Attractive:
Be Discovered

*People are drawn towards
those who understand them.*

How To Become More Attractive

There has been a lot of talk in the marketing and advertising industries about how to make a brand more attractive. Some say that there are specific elements that can make one thing call more attention to your services than others. Others say that attracting crowds is impossible without advanced technology, like artificial intelligence. Yet, another group will say that any actions taken to make an idea draw more attention is futile, as things are what they are, and any effort to draw people in is just manipulation.

I remember a time about ten years ago when I was looking for a job and received an invitation to attend an interview. The day of the interview, I stood in front of the mirror wondering whether I should shave or not before showing up. You see, I have very sensitive skin, so I try not to shave more than once or twice a week, and only under extreme circumstances! Quite frankly, it wasn't that my beard made me look like I was a castaway. I was interviewing with a creative agency, so they might not have cared about something as trivial as the length of my facial hair at all.

In any case, I decided that it was in my best interest to shave, for the simple reason that depending on who I was going to interview with my facial hair could send the wrong message. They might have been more attracted to hire someone that showed up clean cut than someone who didn't even consider their appearance. So, despite my preference, I went ahead and "cleaned my face" as my wife would say. (For the record, my wife doesn't really mind my beard... as long as I don't rub it against her face!) I showed up with a good-looking resumé, a polished cover letter, and I dressed appropriately with cleanly shaved cheeks.

What does shaving before an interview have to do with being found by your market? We are all quite familiar with taking specific actions towards making something more attractive to others. Whether it's through our appearance, when selling a product, or when looking to persuade others about an idea, we know that it's our responsibility to make what we're presenting as appealing as possible for others.

There is one element that we automatically take into consideration in the above scenarios, yet one which we tend to ignore when it comes to developing our personal brand. Because we've been told that it's wrong "to promote ourselves," in situations where we have no other option but to do so, we tend to ignore making ourselves more attractive the way we do with virtually everything else.

The main question behind how to make yourself more attractive is: *Who* are you trying to attract?

In my silly story at the beginning of this chapter, I was looking to attract an employer by using my skills, abilities, and my attention to small details such as my appearance, with the specific outcome of making them interested in hiring me. I wasn't looking to be attractive to everyone in the world, nor was I looking to achieve any outcome possible. I had a very clear objective in mind, and I was looking to make an impression on a very specific individual.

In relation to business, how would you precisely define those you wish to draw nearer to you? Throughout the rest of this chapter, I'll help you answer this question.

Do We Really Need More Visibility?

A s I mentioned a few chapters back, I think that visibility is overrated, or at best, woefully vague. Thousands of people each year become exponentially more visible from one day to another. Do you know who they are? They're the criminals that come out on the 9 o'clock TV news. Yet, nobody wants to become visible in that manner.

If you're looking to grow your business opportunities and feel like you need to become more visible, you might be referring to climbing out of the abyss of obscurity, where nobody except your family members know who you are yet. There might certainly be a benefit in going from total anonymity to getting known by at least *someone*, but this is not what you really want.

Instead of becoming visible, what you are really looking for is to be known as a reliable provider of a specific and valuable service to a very specific audience: people who will either do business with you or who may know people who will do business with you.

A solid personal brand needs to do more than just become visible. It needs to be attractive, and attraction has *everything* to do with *who* we are looking to attract.

My first book, Digital BACON, was published with this subtitle: "Make Your Online Presence Irresistibly Attractive." In that book, I outlined the formula to achieve attraction in digital campaigns for companies, products, and brands.

I'm honored that many people love my book, and although I'm largely proud of it, I regret one thing. You see, throughout the book, I discuss so many ideas and concepts, from research, to strategy, to creativity, and analysis. All good stuff, but the one thing I feel funny about is that the part about "making something irresistibly attractive" might have been difficult to understand for most readers.

Therefore, I feel like in this book, I've been granted a second opportunity to be 100% clear on what goes into making something attractive and I don't intend to squander it!

The recipe to make your brand irresistibly attractive is to connect it with another person's needs or desires by making it highly *relevant* to them, while requiring the least amount of effort on their part to understand how relevant it is to their situation.

Your brand should address people's true needs — not just the needs for your service, but their deep, legitimate needs — and you address them by offering 100% effortless access to the value you bring them. Do this and your power to influence and attract will be impossible to resist.

You might think it's obvious, but if it were, everyone would be applying this to their personal brand. Unfortunately, very few people in business do this today.

The key to making this secret work is to know and understand *who* you are looking to attract so that you can appeal to them through every effort you put forth.

Your Audience Persona

Most people in my field would call the type of person you are looking to attract a "target." Although it's quite an accepted term, the word makes me feel a bit weird. It's almost like I'm throwing darts at the very people I'm trying to serve.

I prefer calling the people we're trying to reach as an "audience." Even by using this term, we risk referring to the idea of a shapeless mass of people. But in my mind, an audience is a group of people with somewhat similar qualities which I'm trying to reach. Each and every one of the people within this group is special and has individual experiences that makes them unique.

To shape your personal brand in a way that will help you address their deepest needs, you must find the similar qualities among them, so that you can then have an idea about how to approach them. Despite these similarities, you'll *never* treat the members in this audience as a soulless blob.

To ensure you're addressing an individual's needs, it helps to develop what I call an Audience Persona. As mentioned in the previous chapter, a Persona is a representation of someone's main qualities and details. Just as in the previous chapter, I'll be using this concept to help you visualize the typical individual who will buy into your business offer, but who will also be attracted to your personal style, your aspects, your story, and other elements we'll discuss later in this book.

> *"You need to know your audience so well that they feel like you've been reading their minds."*

Being attractive depends on knowing your audience deeply, so this effort is critically important. You need to know your audience so well that they feel like you've been reading their minds. They need to feel that you are talking to them, their needs, and their deepest desires.

Let's dig into three ways to describe your audience, which will help us build an Audience Persona.

Demographics

The first thing that is helpful to determine about our audience are their most tangible qualities, which we normally call demographics. People tend to think demographics are important because you'll somehow figure out how they all behave in unison, but this isn't why. The reason you want to figure these out is to find topical commonalities among them, and at the same time, avoid topics that might not be relevant to their common experience.

No matter what you do in business, you are *never* talking to absolutely everyone. You are looking to connect with a very specific type of individual and address their unique needs. Your audience's demographics will get you on your way towards being more in touch with them.

If you were to describe one individual who appreciates what you do and might grant you an opportunity to help them, what would be your description of them?

Read through the list of questions below, and try to answer each one. If you find that any of these questions are a bit difficult, it might be because you need to press on and put in a bit more effort. Take a moment to stop and think a bit more about who it is that you're really looking to connect with.

With this in mind, answer the following questions:

- What age is your audience? (A range is fine, but it's better to peg a specific age in the middle of the range.)
- What is their gender? (Only if it tends to skew more towards one. It's fine to reply "all" if this is accurate.)
- What is their marital status?
- Where do they tend to live?
- What is their household income?
- What is their current employment status?
- In what industry are they employed?
- What is their education level?
- What is their ethnicity/race?
- What is their parental status?
- How many children do they have?

If your mind responded to any of these with, "Yikes, it's all over the place. I work with all kinds of people," then you probably aren't thinking about your *ideal* audience member. While it's true that you might be able to do business with most anyone, it's also true that there is one type of person who you will most likely do business with.

Another way to respond to these questions is to think about one of your best clients. Wouldn't you like to work with more people like them? If so, respond to the questions above with their real descriptions.

Another way to define your audience Persona — particularly if you're just starting out — is by replying to the questions with who your best client *could be*. Of course, you're looking to be realistic here, but what type of person do you honestly dream about serving?

A question I get asked all the time is, "Well, what if I'm selling services to other businesses?" Even in those cases, you are never selling to a "business." You are selling to decision-makers *within* that business.

Therefore, if this is your situation, try to define the typical decision-maker you might encounter in the businesses you wish to sell your services to.

By looking at demographics, we've outlined your target audience's tangible qualities. Let's now move on towards intangible elements of your Audience Persona, which are equally important to define.

Psychographics

In this section, we want to draw a clear picture of the stuff they carry in their hearts and minds which makes them who they are. Why? Because ultimately, we are looking to affect their behavior, which flows from their thoughts, desires, and attitudes. Their actions don't typically flow from where they live nor any of the points we talked about in the previous section.

Demographics and Psychographics achieve very different goals in this exploration. Demographics help you understand their *experience*, whereas Psychographics deal with the person's particular *behaviors and mindset*.

As in the previous section, I'll invite you to look over the following questions and try to see whether you can offer an objective answer for each of them:

- What do people in your objective audience occupy their time with? (You can include outdoor situations, as well as activities within their homes.)

- What topics are they interested in? Another more specific way to phrase the question is: Which publications, TV shows, websites, etc., do they tend to read and view?

- What are their strongest opinions? (Particularly, in relation to something tied to your business)

- What is their outlook on life?

- What is their ethical stance, and what is it based on?

- Are there any recognizable patterns among their actions (above those required for survival)?

Now we're beginning to paint a clearer picture of them as living, breathing, human beings. Just to jog your head even further about your Audience Persona, I want to provide you with one last set of questions that will help make yourself attractive to them:

- What would motivate them to listen to someone like you? Here I want you to go beyond answers like "I know what I'm talking about," "My stuff is good," or "I am certified." They don't care about you, at least not right now. They care about *themselves*. So what motivations do they *already* have?

- Why are they looking for the solution you are offering and why haven't they found it yet? In the very least, why haven't they found something like what you are making available?

- Where would they typically go to solve their problems? Have they attempted to solve them on their own, or do they think about going to a certain type of provider? If there was no solution available in the market, how would they solve it today?

- Since when have they been dealing with this issue? Is it a spur of the moment issue, or is it more of a life-long problem? Do they repeatedly deal with this problem? At what frequency?

- Why are they suffering from this issue? Is it something they got into willingly, by accident, or is it quite a common problem?

- How would they feel if all of a sudden someone were to wipe away their problem? Would they be excited, empowered, healthy, or something else?

These questions are not meant to *inform* you about anything, as I have no idea who you're trying to reach or who you personally connect best with. Rather, I mean to provide you with a guideline to deeply understand who you are looking to connect with, and how what you do connects with their needs.

Technographics

So far we've defined the tangible and intangible aspects of our Audience Persona, and this last section deals with their use of technology. In great measure, the solutions we'll see further along in the book will be digital in nature. We're either going to focus on digital tactics, or leverage digital channels so that our offline and in-person tactics live on much longer and have much more impact. This is why we need to have a clear idea of how a typical member of your audience uses technology.

When people come to me and say, "But my audience doesn't really use technology," I cringe like a sheet of aluminum foil after someone unwraps their sandwich. In some manner or another, everyone worth reaching these days uses some kind of technology. Even if they're not avid and proficient users, they will come into contact with tech in some manner or another.

Now think about your Audience Persona, and see if you can answer these questions:

- What type of devices do they typically use?
- What type of device do they tend *not* to use?
- On which websites would they pick up news and information?
- Which social channels would they use to keep in touch with

friends and family? Which would they use to connect with business peers?

- Are they the type of person that is comfortable purchasing products directly online?

- Which online news outlets give them FOMO (Fear Of Missing Out) when they don't visit them for a day or two, and which others do they care about the least?

- What is their attitude towards reading books and helpful information through electronic devices?

- Do they consume video online?

By answering these, you'll have a clearer idea of how your Audience Persona utilizes technology and how you might be able to reach them in a more scalable manner. You will need to refer to the information in Chapter 8 where we talk about Alignment.

Wrap-Up of Audience Traits

So far we've explored Demographic, Psychographic, and Technographic traits of your ideal Audience Persona. As we mentioned, Demographics help you understand their experience, Psychographics clarify their behaviors and mindset, and Technographics reveal the channels that they invest their attention into, which you can then use to reach them.

Whatever you think you sell is irrelevant if it fails to satisfy a real need or desire in your Audience Persona. When they observe or listen to you, they need to feel like the attention they've invested provides a valuable experience to them in exchange.

One more point: When attracting an audience, it's better to go narrow and deep, than wide and shallow. In other words, it's much better to connect in a profound way with fewer people, than to try to be attractive to a massive audience who will never care to engage deeper with you. We are not trying to become the next pop music celebrity here. We are looking to sell our most precious asset — our own selves — in exchange for their most valuable currency: their individual attention.

Putting On The Gloves

In the previous chapter, we worked on defining your Influential Persona, which is composed of your Aspects, your Personality, and your Story. Just as you went through some of the ideas there and chose what best "fit" your authentic self, your Influential Persona will also be a "fit" for a certain type of audience.

Think of your Influential Persona as a hand. You begin with what you came with from birth, like the lines on your palm or the shape of your fingernails. These are your hand's Aspects. Then look at how you add Personality to your hand, like wearing a ring, painting your fingernails, etc. Finally, your hands have a Story. For example, my right thumb hurts every now and then because I got kicked by a Black Belt in Taekwondo.

If your Influential Persona is like your hand, then your Audience Persona is like the glove that fits around it. If the glove doesn't quite fit, you're either not going to be able to stick your hand inside, or it'll flop out as you move it.

There will be a type of person who will be attracted to a certain type of Influential Persona, and also a type of person that will be repelled by the same Influential Persona. This is just as true with any consistent brand. The more you make your brand concrete and clear, the more you will need to clarify whether they should pay attention to you or not.

In any business development activity, there will be three types of people you can potentially connect with:

1. People who will buy from you
2. People who might buy from you
3. People who won't buy from you

Therefore, when putting your message out into the world, it should achieve three goals:

1. Attract those who will buy from you
2. Provide more clarity to people who might buy from you—so they can decide which of the other two groups they really belong to
3. Repel the people who won't ever buy from you

A way you can begin finding your proper audience fit is through keeping up the activity to attract the first group and repel the third group. In this process, you will notice that the people in the second group will shift towards one group or the other as they receive more clarity about what it is that you do and how you can help them.

How To Fill A Glove With An OCEAN

A nother method to finding a good audience fit has to do with your OCEAN- those big five personality traits you outlined about yourself in the previous chapter. In most situations, you will find that members of an audience are drawn towards people with clarity about who they are and the value they provide, but also who are in a large manner similar to them.

It turns out that opposites do not always attract, and science confirms this. A recent study discovered that people who tend to draw together display very similar traits among them, even when they have barely known each other[7]. In fact, the more a particular trait matters to a person, the more they will seek to relate to people who share that trait. Researchers believe that this phenomenon occurs because relating to people who share our same traits requires less effort, and therefore we tend to put up less resistance against it[8].

---

7 *"New Study Finds Our Desire for 'Like-Minded Others' is Hard-Wired,"* Wellesley College and the University of Kansas, www.wellesley.edu/news/2016/february/node/83586#pkR3UcGjlvTe7M5C.97

8 From research published in the Journal of Personality and Social Psychology, from the American Psychological Association.

Take a glance at your OCEAN chart and give serious thought about how you might be much more successful at attracting people similar to you in each of the five personality traits.

For example, if your personality scores low on the Openness scale — let's say, because you tend to examine an idea deeply with a lot of facts and evidence before considering it, you will most likely attract someone with a similar hesitation to new ideas.

This is quite reasonable. If you display low openness, not only will you require lots of proof before you accept something as fact, but you'll also tend to provide a good amount of proof when you express any new ideas. Therefore, you'll attract people who normally apply a similar level of scrutiny towards new ideas, and at the same time, you'll probably repel a section of people who might get easily saturated with too much intellectual evidence and not enough emotional motivation.

Attracting Through Consistency

K nowing who you're trying to reach is only half of what will help make you more attractive to this audience. The other half has to do with the value you're giving them in exchange.

Your personal brand's power to influence grows based on how consistent you are in delivering this value. It is absolutely impossible to become attractive by simply dipping your toes in the pond and then running away. You need to take the dive, immerse yourself into the idea that you are selling yourself and the way you assist others, and therefore need to be showing up at all times.

We live in a culture where fast results, instant returns, and the desperation people feel when working on raising their profile is normal. People usually want to perform a couple of tricks and quickly get the results they've always wanted, or abandon the project altogether. However, that's not ever going to work because the world is full of many people superficially dabbling in every little thing while making a bit of noise here and there.

If becoming attractive were as easy as just putting in minimal effort and then letting go, everyone would be doing it; but if everyone were doing it, then it would be impossible to stand out. You need to be consistent with your brand. It isn't easy work, but the outcome will position you as someone who is willing to put in the hard work and is therefore worthy of the reward. It will differentiate you from those others who will always be busy chasing after clients while trying to put in the least amount of effort into their brand.

In the end, you are a provider of solutions, and these solutions don't come from random places. If I need to twist a screw, I don't take my entire toolbox and throw it on top of it. I pick up the one single tool that will predictably do the job.

If you want to be the solution that people think about right when they need it the most, you need to show up as such each and every time. Your new goal is to become so visible, attractive, and consistent that the solution your audience sees in their mind is the one that you offer.

The Snowball Effect

What I'm told by people who have much more experience living in places where it snows, is that when you're by a slope or mountain, and the snow reaches a certain level of humidity and consistency, if you pack the snow with your hands into a nice, compact ball and throw it down the slope, the ball will roll downward picking up more and more snowflakes. As it approaches the bottom, it will end up being larger than the ball you originally formed with your hands.

Many people go forth with their brand as if just dropping snowflakes. They perform one or two actions, get busy on other things, get back to it whenever they remember to, and then abandon the whole project.

> "It's not about the snowflakes; it's all about the snowball."

Don't fool yourself. It's not about the snowflakes; it's all about the snowball.

Each action you take to make your personal brand more attractive is like a snowflake. As long as you are consistently on track, you are generating an immense cumulative effect. You're looking to create a humongous, rolling snowball of impressively consistent activity to such a degree that it becomes impossible for people looking for your type of help to ignore you.

If you came to this book thinking that developing your personal brand included an introductory period where without much commitment, you'd be able to tell whether it works or it doesn't, I'm very sorry to disappoint you. To be attractive, you have to fully immerse yourself within a permanent and unending practice of providing value, showing your interest in connecting with others, and giving them reasons why they should pay you with their attention. You must show up and take action as frequently as possible with the same exact mission in mind.

You are your business' most valuable asset, and selling will become a piece of cake after you are able to close this first Transaction of Attention. Being inconsistent about growing your personal brand — that is, working on it one day, and then getting back to it whenever you remember to do so — is pretty much like having a store without set business hours, and instead, being open whenever the you feel like it. Would you be able to build any kind of sales projection off of a business that operates this way? Of course not.

This is exactly what happens when people dabble their toes into something as important as their brand, yet never commit fully to the task at hand. They are never able to achieve a concrete idea of their personal brand's power to influence because that power simply has not been generated. It has been diluted every time they abandoned the task. It was lost within the gaps and peaks when they were too busy or too apathetic to keep working on generating a consistent expectation through consistent activity.

Beginning today, you will keep your eye on that growing snowball, while you work every single day on the snowflakes of small tasks and actions required.

Creating Your "Signature"

An aspect that will help you be consistent in your brand is to develop unique ways to perform certain tasks in the same exact manner every time.

When you sign a blank check, you are expected to sign it in a consistently similar manner each time. Your signature is expected to be a representation of your identity. It's expected — or maybe even inevitable — that your signature shows some aspect of your personality. It is also expected that your signature not be a copy of someone else's.

This concept of a signature can also carry over to other things you do. For example, when I end my emails, instead of writing a cold "Regards" or "Sincerely," I consistently type the words "All the best" before my name. This is my unique way of hoping the other person receives the very best in their lives, which is a sincere desire on my part. It also subliminally impresses a high standard of excellence in our experience of interacting together. In other words, our conversation should be all about striving for the best of the best from both ends.

Floyd Mayweather Jr., the legendary boxing star, begins all of his press conferences screaming "HARD WORK!" while his crew responds

"DEDICATION!" and he does it again at least three more times. It's his way of "signing" that moment with his unique values of hard work and dedication in his sport.

Mark Zuckerberg, the CEO of Facebook, shows up to all of his conferences in a graphite gray t-shirt and jeans. When asked about why he does this, he replied, "I really want to clear my life to make it so that I have to make as few decisions as possible about anything except how to best serve this community." Whether you agree with his decision or not, he is attempting to communicate one of his values through his choice to not wear anything other than a graphite gray t-shirt and jeans.

The reason developing signatures helps grow your attraction is because it helps others develop an expectation of who you are and how you show up. You see, it might take more than one contact for people to get familiar with your unique brand. If every contact with you is a different experience, it becomes quite difficult to form a concrete idea of how you intend to be perceived and remembered.

By developing and utilizing your signatures, you help drill into people's minds the elements that make you unique. Some of the actions you may want to consider when developing your signature are:

- The way you address people when picking up the phone
- The way you sign your emails and letters
- The way you end your videos and livestreams
- The colors you use in social media posts and graphics
- The fonts you use in your proposals and invoices
- The way you shake people's hands at events
- Your pose and hand gestures when someone takes a picture of you

Take some time and think about how you currently perform these and other common tasks, and whether you can begin doing them in a predictably unique manner that identifies you.

Playing Your Own Game

Many times we get exhausted in our pursuit to become more attractive in our industry because we see other people who are more popular, more distinguished, and have a larger audience than we have. You might feel stunned when you observe that other players in your field are just so much farther ahead of you. They're the keynote speakers, the best-selling authors, and the ones who get invited to consultations and partnership opportunities. The sheer intimidation might cause you to be paralyzed and stay in the same place.

This thought is utterly, completely, and absolutely fallacious. Business is not a race. There is no medal or championship cup at the end of the track for the business that generates the most revenue or closes more sales. Even if you are in a sales department where they issue awards and bonuses to keep employees motivated, you are still playing your own game.

> *"Playing someone else's game only leads to disappointment."*

In your game, you declare your own rules, confront your own monsters, and receive rewards and penalties according to how hard you've worked or refused to make an effort.

Playing *someone else's* game only leads to disappointment. You see them so far ahead of you that you feel left behind. But here's the deal: They aren't playing *your* game, so why should you be playing theirs? People who have a strong personal brand are only focused on their own game, not yours.

This is one of the secret keys of attraction: Those who have a defined purpose and seem to have it "together" tend to be more attractive than people who seem to be figuring things out as they go along. Small children early on learn to rely on parents who seem to have a concrete set of guidelines around their actions, their rules, and their behaviors. Even as adults, we haven't abandoned this tendency to gravitate towards people who stand solidly for something.

The way to show that you have a defined purpose and a solid idea of where you're going is by playing your own game consistently.

From this moment, and until you gain traction on your personal brand, don't even pay attention to where others are or what they are doing. Later on, when things begin rolling, you can look outwards to form new alliances, but for now, looking outward at what your competitors are doing won't help you one bit.

The We/Me Paradox

Another trap of playing other people's game that tends to get people stuck is when they see audiences as an amorphous mass of human matter. They see others who have larger numbers in their audience than what they have, bigger lists, more followers, etc.

Do you want to know something that irks me? People getting on a social channel like Instagram and addressing their followers like this: "Hi Instagram!" *Seriously?!* Not only are they treating people like they don't even have their own identities, they're referring to them as if *they* are all tiny people living inside an app!

This is a terrible way to think about connecting with others. Individuals in the audience never see themselves as part of a mass of people; they see themselves as individual human beings with very particular needs and desires.

Think about it. When you've looked towards someone to ask for their solutions, insights, or advice, how much time did you spend thinking about which "audience" you belong to? I would dare to say you spent zero time or mental energy on such a silly question. You usually just think about what you need at that moment, and about who could solve it. Yet, so many people working on their personal brand seem to get stumped by this.

When people are looking for a solution, they don't wonder what "audience" they're in. They look outwards for someone who can solve their particular problem. People never see themselves as a "we" but only as a "me."

When I talk on stage or go to book signings, people tend to come by to take pictures with me or to ask me a question. I usually greet them with a hug and ask their name. I do my best to connect with that one person, and I do it sincerely with every single person I meet. If they post their picture with me on a social channel and tag me, I do my best to reply with a comment saying that it was great to connect or something along those lines, and I really mean it. For me, it's an amazing privilege to be able to connect deeply with one individual.

The number of people you connect with only matters when you are taking mechanical and cold actions, like building sales projections and closing rates. It absolutely doesn't matter when measuring your power to attract or figuring out how deeply you are connecting with every single person.

Therefore, begin approaching your brand as if your goal is to attract only **one** "me" and not a large "we."

Here's the surprising truth about thinking this way: the actions you take to become attractive to **one** ideal individual will automatically attract more and more people similar to them as well.

> *"When you focus on one, you attract many. When you focus on many, it's hard to attract one in a meaningful way."*

When you focus on one, you attract many. When you focus on many, it's hard to attract one in a meaningful way. This is what I call the We/Me Paradox.

I consistently apply this idea in the way I write. I never write to "all of you." I know thousands of people will read these words, but I never speak to the thousands. No, I'm talking to you. You were attracted to read this book because you knew I'd be talking about *your* interests and concerns on a very personal level.

People who have read snippets of this book have already told me *"I felt you were talking about me."* The reason I know I can talk about you is that I've done my research. I know where you are and where you want to be in your professional and business life. Therefore, you were attracted to read this book as soon as you saw the cover and haven't stopped reading because you can agree that what I have been discussing relates to you in a very deep way.

I'm using my relationship between us both — you as a reader and me as the author — as an example of how to do the same thing: speak deeply to one person who is willing to pay their attention, and speak to their very particular needs and desires.

Allow people to be attracted to you through your voice, your tone, and your approach as you talk to them individually, and they will want to move closer to hear more of what you can say to help them in their lives or their businesses.

Final Thoughts on Attraction

So far, we've seen what it takes to make your personal brand become authentically grounded in who you are, and how to forge a much more attractive brand for yourself. In summary, being Attractive is about knowing people deeply, understanding what they're looking for, and connecting deeply with those needs.

Now it's time to hop on over into the next element of a successful personal brand for your business: Alignment.

CHAPTER 8

Alignment: Value, Brand, Buyer

Value is made clear at every touchpoint of a brand's presence.

What Does Alignment Mean?

Back when I was still in high school, I had a dream of becoming a full-time musician. In fact, I actually did reach this dream, as during the first few years out of school, it's all I did as a profession. Through music, I was able to pay for my college tuition and even support my recently widowed mother as much as I could.

I played pretty much anything, from jazz to cheesy elevator music, but deep inside, I wanted to be known as a rock musician. I bought a keyboard you can strap on as you would with a guitar — popularly known as a "keytar." I even made up some tapping techniques on the pitch bend touchstrip that sounded a lot like the amazing tapping runs that Van Halen or Yngwie Malmsteen used to do on stage…at least it sounded like that to me!

I developed such a rock 'n' rollers' heart, that at one point, I began sneering at music that sounded too "soft" — even though I'd secretly play that exact music at weddings! In any case, when I was in front of my rock-loving friends, I would call that music "Basura," which means "Garbage" in Spanish.

Well, I guess I repeated the word so much that my friends started calling me "Basura" and it was eventually seared onto me as a nickname. I still have many friends to this day who call me "Garbage." I have to admit, I really liked the name back then! It was raw, full of angst and disregard for what others thought about me. I thought it was great!

I embraced that brand for many years…but then something happened. I stepped into the advertising world, and started working in the visual identity field among agencies and global brands with their strict guidelines and top tier executives. I kept using my brand, because "Basura" was all I knew and all I had developed until that point. Unfortunately, that brand had absolutely zero alignment with the new field I was suddenly thrust into.

One day I was discussing about becoming part of the crew on one of the hottest film directors in the advertising world back then, and he stopped to question me. "Garbage?" he asked, with a tone of concern. "Does that have something to do with the quality of your work, or with you as a person?"

The reality is that it had to do with neither of the two, so the brand was doing no favors for me. It wasn't communicating anything aligned with how I wanted to be perceived at that point in my career, and worse yet, it was probably communicating the exact opposite of what I wanted people to expect. They didn't associate "Garbage" with someone they would consider hiring for a high-level advertising project in which they were investing millions of dollars and expected only the best of results.

Needless to say, I had to find a way to scrap that brand and start from scratch. For over twenty years, I have never once introduced myself with that nickname to someone I'm meeting for the first time.

Why Alignment?

Whether you had a nickname that means something undesirable like I did, or have just let the winds blow you around and now you're not even sure whether your current brand may support your business goals, you might have felt a similar struggle. You may have even been so frustrated with this tension that you've questioned whether having a personal brand is useful or even valuable.

The hard truth is that your brand can be highly attractive. It can also be authentically tied to your true essence as a person. Even in these cases, it can still be completely without value as a business asset because it fails to support your actual goals in business. The way to ensure that it *will* support your business is by working on your brand's alignment.

Who you are and what you do in your business are, and should continue to be, two separate things. You are not your business, and your business will never be an inseparable part of your true being. Yet, as separate as they are, you need to ensure that a straight line can still be drawn between the two.

Otherwise, if it's hard for people to connect what you stand for as a person with the business value you can bring, this whole exercise of developing your brand will never help bring your name into the mind of someone looking for your services.

In this chapter, I'm going to show you how to reach this level of complete alignment between who you are and what you desire to accomplish in your business.

Your Main Value Proposition

After going to many business meetings and countless networking groups, if you asked me what is the #1 thing people in business are failing at, it has to be the way they present their value. There are two types of intro statements you generally hear. It's either Insecure Irene:

"I…you know…I'm an accountant…and, well…I kinda do accounting."

Or it's Salesman Sal:

"I represent XYZ Corp. and I sell insurance policies. Here's my business card!"

Nobody wants to hear you wade through your insecurities, and they certainly don't want to you to sell to them upon first meeting you. What people **love** to hear about is how you are able to help other people.

It is vital that you learn to express the value that you bring to others through a clear, concise statement. I'm not talking about a long, drawn-out pitch. You just need one sentence that every time you speak it, it allows others to clearly understand what you do and who you do it for.

You can't go wrong with the following template, which you can take 5 minutes to fill out now:

"My name is _____A_____, and I help _____B_____ with _____C_____, without _____D_____ or _____E_____."

In this template:

A - Your name.

B - The type of person you help (a short description of what you came up with as your Audience Persona).

C - The kind of help you offer. Make it about the benefit they *receive* and not so much about the actions you take.

D and E - Common objections people have when considering your type of solution, which you can distinguish your service from. (These are optional, but they really help clarify what you do.)

As this chapter deals with aligning everything you do with the value you bring, it is imperative that you keep your Main Value Proposition statement in mind at all times.

The reason people lose Alignment and become irrelevant as they build their personal brand is either that their ego gets in the way, or they simply get distracted about their business' end goal. A clear Main Value Proposition will help you keep focus on:

a) How you manage to help others (as opposed to speaking only about what benefits you).

b) How everything else you do branches out from the ideas you deeply believe in.

As a side effect, you'll also help others deeply understand how you are prepared to support them.

The Elusive Entry Point

From the beginning of this book, we've been focusing on the Transaction of Attention, which far precedes our sales appointments. Improving the volume and quality of the first type of transaction will generate more of the second kind. To ensure our brand is as aligned as possible, it's important to define exactly how this second kind of transaction takes place. One of the most serious oversights when building your brand is having zero connection to what I call a business' "Entry Point."

First, let me define what I mean by "Entry Point." Quite simply, it's the initial action a person is required to take when engaging with you or your business. All businesses have an Entry Point, and some have multiple ones. Some begin with an initial phone call, a walk-in to their facilities, an email inquiry, an initial session, among others.

At our firm, our general Entry Point is a free 30-minute Discovery Session. People can use a tool to book whichever day and time is best in their own calendar, without having to play email ping-pong or calling unannounced and interrupting each other. We also have a questionnaire that we go through, which we've used hundreds of times. Before the meetings, I can tell exactly how long it will take to go through everything, because I've gone through this process so many times with hundreds of businesses.

We have another Entry Point, which is a 1-hour Strategy Session. We offer this session for people who would like to understand whether they should invest in digital marketing or not. This is a paid session, but we also offer it for free in exchange for a small donation to a local non-profit organization. We have defined precisely what to expect at these meetings, and we know exactly what people walk away with after meeting with us.

Unfortunately, most consultative professionals never develop their personal brand with their Entry Point in mind. They are completely lost in the woods about such a simple concept. For example, they will publish articles every now and then, just because they've heard that it's good to "get your name out there." Aside from the articles having zero relevance to their Main Value Proposition, neither do they have the slightest invitation to their Entry Point.

The most likely reason why there is hardly any invitation to an Entry Point is because they feel like having one would be "pushy." It's just wrong to sell, they say. This is just a symptom of a severe lack of alignment. If it ever feels dirty to bring up your Entry Point through anything you're doing, it might be because of one of these two:

a) Your activities to "put yourself out there" have absolutely nothing to do with your business value, so bringing up your Entry Point feels abrasive and full of friction.

I like to call this problem "willful irrelevance." Other people know them as a devoted political analyst, a fan of a certain sports team, a film critic, anything except a professional who can solve a particular problem.

Therefore, it's natural for them to feel inappropriate when mentioning their business.

There is always a right time and place to bring up your Entry Point, but most people lock themselves out of all places and allow themselves no time to do business by creating irrelevant conversations rather than aligned ones.

b) Your Entry Point sounds cumbersome and has not been well-defined. In the minds of others, it takes too much effort to engage with you.

This problem has to do with refusing to create exceptional and frictionless experiences towards your business' Entry Point. If engaging with you sounds too difficult or cumbersome, the decision to engage with you is probably going to be put off for another day.

The way to overcome these issues is simple. You need to have a well-defined Entry Point that makes sense for your business, which doesn't feel like a chore when you present it to others, and is something you can align your brand-building efforts toward.

Is your Entry Point an initial session? An application to your program? A valuable in-person meeting? How much time does it take? What are the exact steps they need to take to engage with this activity? Do they need to have a certain device or application to do so? How many resources do you or your team need to dedicate toward each person who approaches you?

It is absolutely necessary for you to define each and every aspect of your Entry Point. Otherwise, your presentation will not be clear, and your lack of clarity will only breed lack of action in others.

Content as Products

As I mentioned a few chapters back, people today expect value way before any type of monetary transaction takes place. This flies against every notion of business we have been accustomed to for centuries, but it's the reality of our day; and you can either kick, scream, and fight against it, or embrace it and take advantage of the immense opportunities to differentiate yourself from those people kicking and screaming.

Consumers today are looking for value, and more specifically, valuable products. But what is a "product" anyway? When we think of products, we think about labeled boxes on a shelf or items we can order from an online store. However, marketing textbooks define a product as "that which satisfies a need or desire in the mind of a consumer." It doesn't say anything about a box, a shopping cart, or an online store.

All that a product needs to do is fulfill someone's need or desire at a particular moment, and their investment in that product doesn't have to require them to pull out their wallet or credit card. Products can be paid for with the currency of attention.

With this in mind, a product can be aligned and valuable information intended to help a certain type of person at a certain point in their lives. This type of product offers numerous advantages:

a) **Content products are scalable**. Producing valuable information can be a one-time effort that satisfies many people.

b) **Content is affordable.** Giving your products or your time away to each person who inquires about you without any monetary transaction might not be sustainable. On the other hand, providing value through content costs a fraction of the price of your time and other resources.

c) **Content has value.** When you give away information that helps a person in your ideal audience, you are giving them the gift of an easier life situation, of quickly overcoming a business obstacle, or some other benefit whereby they can remember you.

> "Content is the pathway, not the final destination."

The key to content-as-products, specifically towards building your brand and elevating your profile, is that it must be connected to *you*, to who you are as a person. Content is the pathway, not the final destination. This is the link that ties the previous chapters with this one, so I'll say it in a different way: The content you share needs to be as much a connection between your ideal audience and your business topic, as well as the unique manner these two connect to you.

Let's take the case of an HR consultant. She decides to develop an article about how to fire an employee, as she's identified that topic often makes HR directors and business owners anxious. She has developed five steps that every company needs to follow to reduce the stress of the situation and avoid affecting the rest of their workforce negatively.

An article about the topic that is not grounded in their personal brand might be informative and helpful, and may connect their target audience with value, but it will be lacking the key element that ties everything together: establishing *her* authority in the subject, which will have a greater chance of generating inquiries and consultation requests.

It's much more powerful to have an article that speaks about the same five steps towards firing compassionately, written by a person who speaks from the value of Authenticity that they already worked from. Imagine that the HR consultant gave her Influential Persona the personality of a Humble Hero, and her story uses the "Us vs. Them" framework. Their article might begin somewhat like this:

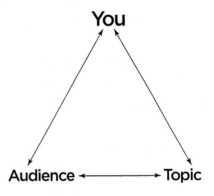

"In this article, I would love to share some very helpful insights to help keep your workforce motivated, particularly in the face of a largely negative event such as the sudden termination of one of your employees. I stumbled upon a 5-step process after making many mistakes when firing employees. I must be sincere here: I was once one of those people who didn't think twice before firing an employee abruptly."

"Like ripping off a bandage from one's skin, I wanted to get over the painful experience quickly and get along with more important matters. I also thought the morale recovery process was pretty simple, but boy, was I wrong."

"Yes, I was once one of those heartless corporate butchers, but I've learned my lesson. During the past 15 years I've become part of a global movement that strongly believes that if you must let an employee go, you can do so while still being compassionate and treating people with dignity. I've developed five steps towards achieving just that, which I'm thrilled to share with you below…"

See how that sounds? It has such a balanced measure of sharing helpful information while establishing a humble yet helpful personality. It also shares the story of how they began standing in contrast against a type of attitude that they used to belong to, but now criticize openly.

An intro like this *may* turn off people just looking to pick up straight-to-the-point information, and that's perfectly fine because *those aren't the people you're looking to connect with!* The person in this example is looking to give people value, but specifically, they are looking to establish their authority and credibility as a consultant. An intro like this is built specifically to appeal to someone looking for an experienced person to hold them by the hand and help them ease a particular pain.

Does Sharing Content Make You Replaceable?

An objection to the notion around sharing your most valuable ideas that often comes up is that giving away information is risky, because you'd be giving away your "secret sauce," your best insights and processes, and therefore, others will never hire you as consultative professionals.

This is a useless thought for several reasons:

1. This concern assumes that the content you can share is not already out there. The truth is that pretty much everything has been said in one manner or another. Heck, even the ideas in this book can be found in snippets out there in the world. The main difference is that it hasn't been said by *you*.

2. The concern also assumes that the value is all about the content, when it's really not. It's about how *you* personally deliver it—provided that you have worked on being Attractive and Authentic.

3. It is based on ignoring that the value people are willing to pay for in today's market is in how you are able to adapt your knowledge to their particular situation and help them implement it.

When I wrote Digital BACON, my first book, some well-intentioned friends warned me that I might be giving too much away. After all, I outlined the exact way I think when developing successful digital campaigns. I gave away all my secrets at the time. Still, my friends' warning didn't make me hesitate, as I strongly believed in sharing most everything I knew and time proved me right. Since its publication date, I have never come upon one potential client who has said, "We were thinking about hiring you as a consultant, but we just downloaded the ebook edition of your book for $5.95. Thanks a lot, but we'll take it from here!"

Even if someone did say that, they'd be removing themselves from my audience on their own. Why? Because I'm not looking to get consultation requests from companies that are convinced that they can do everything on their own just by reading a book or two. This is a company that will **never** be interested in hiring someone like me. I could meet with them for 15 sales appointments and they would still never hire me, so why be concerned?

At the same time, a client with whom I *would* want to connect will look up information and then realize that they need a bit more to get the solution implemented. They love the information, but they need help towards solving their problem. What better way to identify those types of companies than to provide value to them and establish my particular way of delivering that value, way before the appointment to consult with them is even set.

Shaking The Idea Tree

One of the main roadblocks entrepreneurs and consultants face is to come up with ideas to produce content products. They are so close to their subject of expertise, and have so many topics to choose, that they are simply stumped on where to begin.

I like to think about the process of generating content ideas as a large tree that, instead of producing fruit, produced unique and delicious ideas hanging from its branches.

When we operate within a mindset that ideas are scarce and that everyone in our industry is saying the same thing, it becomes very difficult to produce new takes on our topic of expertise to differentiate ourselves. Yet, when we think about content ideas as growing as a tree from our deep and particular manner of seeing our audience's interests, there is really no limit to angles around helpful tips we can generate. Below you'll find my four-step process to generate an endless number of content topics.

Root Ideas

Our Idea Tree is firmly planted in the ground by our root ideas, a fundamental understanding about your audience. It could be a particular aspect about the pain they experience before they work with you, or a specific need that nobody seems to be satisfying. Whatever it is, it must be an undisputable reality about the problem you solve.

A solid Root Idea absolutely *must* be about something that your business can solve. To grow an Idea Tree from a root that has nothing to do with your business is the perfect way to fall into irrelevance. You should begin with something that connects with your business.

Examples:

- "I wish I didn't have to pay so much in taxes each year."

- "It's so hard to access capital when you most need it."

- "There is hardly any support for homeschooling parents."

THE TRUNK

From the Root Idea, we need to build a solid structure to grow your valuable content topics. Just as a strong trunk is the base of a healthy tree, our Trunk will be the foundation for the rest of the steps we'll take.

Take the problem you described in your Root Idea, and re-phrase it from the vantage point of how your business could solve it. We are still stating the problem, just with an obvious connection to your business offer.

Just as the root of a tree remains is mostly concealed in the ground, your root idea might be a concept you keep only in notebooks and whiteboards; however, the Trunk takes that root concept and forms it into phrases and visuals you can begin to use in your surveys and presentations.

In the advertising world I come from, these Trunks are often called "campaign concepts" or "core creative ideas." We often show two or three Trunks to a client, and alongside them will present the Root Ideas that support them: the rationale, research, findings, and other notions that backed it up. In almost every case, we select the best idea not only based on the quality of the Trunk, but two other factors as well: which is the Root Idea closest to reality and which Root-Trunk connection seems most solid.

Examples:

- "Companies are looking for help to avoid paying excessively in taxes."

- "Quick and easy access to capital is essential for a business' sustainability."

- "Eager and busy homeschooling parents are constantly looking for support to do a better job with their child's education."

BRANCHING OFF

Our Idea Tree doesn't end there. Once we know we've grown a solid Trunk, our next task is to extend its Idea Branches.

So far, you've pointed out a problem your audience experiences and have connected it to your business. What is one way in which we could address it? Furthermore, how can we add value to them right at this moment through helpful information? Each answer to these questions will branch off into a content topic.

These will be natural extensions of our core creative idea, our Idea Trunk. How does this understanding apply to different stages of interest from our audience? How does it look like at different budget levels that our products might apply to? Which tips can we offer to appeal to different phases in our customer life cycle?

By branching off into topics, we'll be creating content that explores our main subject from different angles. Our target audience is dynamic, and therefore their interests change all the time. By having a diverse number of angles from which to view your subject, you'll have a bit of something for everyone.

Speaking about the same topic from different angles allows you to establish your authority much more deeply. Think about it: A person who is a newbie at what they do may only be able to repeat their same exact recommendation again and again. On the other hand, we expect that if someone is highly knowledgeable about their subject, they should be able to branch off a main topic into numerous directions, examining and exploring their subject of expertise from many different points of view.

Examples:

- "5 Ways To Avoid Paying Too Much In Tax This Year"
- "3 Creative Methods To Access Capital Right When You Need It"
- "Ten Tips To Support Busy Homeschooling Parents"

PICKING THE FRUITS

Now that we've grown our tree, it's time to harvest! You need to break down your content topic into chunks, actionable tips, insights, or methods to begin solving your audience's issues. Each chunk of advice is a "Fruit" produced from your Idea Tree, which you will then flesh out through descriptions, case studies, and examples.

Develop each Fruit, and then string a few of them together into your main content topic, along with an introduction and a conclusion/call to action.

The easiest thing to do from here is to form our ideas into consumable media. This can be anything, such as:

- Articles
- White Papers
- Case Studies
- Press Releases
- Long-form Videos
- Short-form Videos

- Livestream Videos
- Infographics
- Serial Videos
- Pamphlets
- Newsletters
- Printed brochures
- Books
- Magazines
- Journals
- Blog posts
- Social media posts
- Webinars
- Keynote speeches
- Ebooks
- Workshops
- Courses

Whereas your audience may only ever see the Fruits they are consuming and never the Tree, there is a world of difference between a Fruit that comes from a solid Idea Tree, and content that comes out of nowhere that has no backing, zero substance, and in the end doesn't demonstrate the Alignment we're seeking.

EXAMPLE OF AN IDEA TREE

Here's an Idea Tree that could work for a business financial consultant. Although this may not be your field, for now, just focus on how we could build a relevant Idea Tree for this industry from scratch.

Let's say our Root Idea is that businesses are often left depleted of cash reserves because their invoices aren't in order. This is the unchanging truth that has been observed, and that the consultant *knows for sure* they can help with by providing their services.

From this Root Idea, we grow a Trunk: the reason their invoicing system is broken is due to poor records management and systems. The Trunk can be expressed as a short pitch statement:

"Businesses often deplete their cash reserves due to poor records management and systems for their invoices, which if solved can maintain the business' cash flow steadily."

From there, we can branch the idea out in many different directions, such as:

- Five simple ways to keep clean invoicing records

- Tips to choose between net 15, net 30, and net 60

- Why businesses need an invoice tracking system

- Four advantages of having multiple payment gateways available

- Three ways to handle recurring payments

- When and when not to tap into a factoring service

We can now grow some Fruit from each of these Branches. Take just one of the branches, "ways to handle recurring payments." From this branch, you can outline the actual tips to handle these payments. Then you can bunch these fruits up into one or all of the following:

- A series of short 3-minute videos, each explaining one method

- A "listicle"—an article in the form of a list—with an explanation of each method, and links to resources

- A 1-hour webinar walking businesses step by step through the methods and how to set them up

- A 900 x 2,500 pixel infographic with iconography and a quick explanation on each of the recurring payment methods

- A livestreaming video explaining the methods and a screen share of software tools to set them up

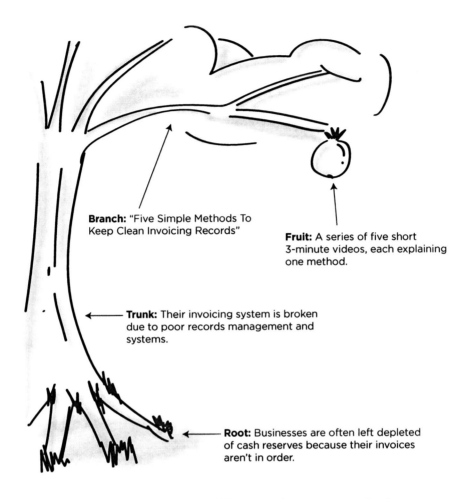

Branch: "Five Simple Methods To Keep Clean Invoicing Records"

Fruit: A series of five short 3-minute videos, each explaining one method.

Trunk: Their invoicing system is broken due to poor records management and systems.

Root: Businesses are often left depleted of cash reserves because their invoices aren't in order.

Now you can see the vast difference between producing content exclusively to "sell yourself as a financial consultant" — which always comes across as pushy and trite — and my Idea Tree approach. This is a much richer way to do it, because as you've seen, it allows you to demonstrate Alignment based on the wide number of angles you can knowledgeably speak from about your subject of specialization.

Selecting Your Content Topics

Before you go off into happy farmer mode, growing Fruit from your new Idea Tree, I want to share some additional tips with you.

Business owners and professionals tend to experience difficulty around telling their story to the outside world. They are typically so engrossed in their day-to-day operations that everything about what they do seems so boring to themselves, and the mere idea of speaking about what they do to the outside world seems like a grueling thought.

I often meet professionals in widely different fields — from attorneys, to real estate agents — for a cup of coffee to hear about what they do each day. Although I've developed a career within the creative environment, I am utterly fascinated to hear about people's wildly different challenges and how they manage to overcome them.

No matter how boring you think what you do is, the people who will place value in what you do can not only find what you do interesting, they may think it's fascinating and even fundamental to their lives or businesses. I'll even go so far as to say that *only* those who will ever consider what you do valuable will be interested in hearing more about it.

You may have doubts on where to even begin. I'm sure your daily routines are astonishingly complex and you might feel like you're not in the business of teaching other people to do what you do. However, here are some idea starters to help you select topics that will attract and retain the attention of people interested in your services.

PRE-EMPTING OBJECTIONS

You surely have heard concerns people have expressed when sitting with you as you go over a proposal or right before they're about to sign one of your contracts. These are some of the questions you might frequently receive at your sales appointments:

- Questions around quality: "How good is this really?" "How much will it really improve my business?" "What if I'm not satisfied?"

- Questions around price: "Why is this priced this way?" "Why is your price higher/lower than your competitors?" "What if I don't have all the money right now? What will the lower-priced option get me?"

- Questions around status: "What makes this more unique than all of the other options?" "Is this really going to place me at the level of my peers/competitors or even beyond?"

Think about questions you've heard at the negotiation table, even if just once before, and write them down on a list. By developing content around each of these, you'll be accomplishing several things at a time.

First, you're shedding light on a topic that is a common concern before they buy into your offer. This in itself is invaluable for people during their research phase, and they will appreciate the extra help while they're making a decision.

Also, by consuming your information, they'll realize that you have no problem addressing these concerns in an open forum, which in turn, will make people feel relieved and more at ease around getting in touch with you. By openly speaking about concerning matter, you show that you have nothing to hide and are actually quite okay with speaking about reasons people choose not to do business with you.

INCREASING ATTRACTION

You can make your professional value more attractive to others by speaking in ways that show that you are in the business of benefiting them in very clear, concrete manners. We often feel afraid to talk about what we do, but that's because we're so focused on *how* we do things that we forget to enhance and draw the details around *why* we do it.

People don't want to hear how you use a spreadsheet application, but they would be thrilled to hear some tips to help a business save 10% or more in taxes this year. They would throw tomatoes at you if you talked about replacing outdated communication technologies, but a story about how a business' operation can be twice as efficient just by looking into their office's technology can make a performance-focused CEO perk up on his or her leather seat.

RESPONDING TO INTEREST

Next time someone approaches you and asks a question about your services, consider that there may be tens, if not hundreds, of others just like them who are wondering the exact same thing. By developing content that responds to these questions, you'll be enriching people's lives by increasing their curiosity and their satisfaction of arriving at the response they needed.

COMPARING OTHER OPTIONS

One of the biggest time investments on the part of people who are "in the market" for a certain service has to do with comparing every option available out there. I've literally spent hours taking notes and comparing pros and cons before I decide to invest in the service that a particular provider could perform for me.

You can help take on a bit of this burden by publishing content that helps potential clients see the differences between each option they have available. Of course, in many instances they will think, "*Of course* you think you're the best option," and take your advice with a grain of salt. However, a good number of these people will probably be happy about the fact that you've saved some of their time by highlighting precisely what makes your offer different from the rest.

INDUSTRY FACTS AND STATS

One of the ways to increase your authority before even presenting your offer is to talk about data and facts regarding your industry. This helps people in several ways, one of the most important being that you are helping curate content for them and feed it to them in reasonable, bite-sized chunks.

You would be filtering through the massive number of sources and highlighting exactly what people should pay attention to at any given time. This has tremendous value, because these days there are simply too many signals competing for our scarce attention. When you curate exactly which pieces of information are important for your audience, you are offering them an incredible service as you help them save their valuable time. Therefore, you become worth the attention they are paying you.

Furthermore, facts and stats don't have to be expressed merely as flat numbers, but rather colored with your interpretation of what they mean, from the standpoint of a true specialist in your field. You're not just barking the same old stats and numbers as anyone else could; you are a commentator, a critic, and an analyst. You are able to give your editorial opinion on your industry, on the market, and on how people can make a wise investment.

The Product Staircase

Many people recommend you build your authority just by giving content away, while others tell you to leave all of this aside and just present people with your offer all the time. Both of these approaches are completely misguided, and dedicating any bit of your resources to either of them will be the greatest waste of your time and energy.

We've already explained why the latter approach doesn't work in our current economy: People expect value well before any monetary transaction takes place. Yet, the former approach doesn't work either. The law of reciprocity, although powerful, will only take you so far. You can give content away all you want, but if you don't begin showing others the path towards engaging deeper and doing business with you, all of this will be in vain. You will only be a voice parroting facts and noise, not a specialist taking a stance and offering deeper value to those who wish to engage with you.

Below, I'll show you a much better system, which I call The Product Staircase. It is based on five types of Content Products, with the notion that people prefer to travel along a gradual journey towards knowing, liking, and trusting someone, before deciding to do business with them.

Let's talk about each one:

The Gift

Objectives

- Gives the potential client a "taste" of the value that we offer if and when they decide to hire us.

- Solves a problem that our potential client has, in a very simple way and without commitment on their part.

- Helps increase your appeal in the eyes of a potential client.

- Increases the knowledge of your personal brand.

This is the type of content that immediately comes to mind whenever we discuss marketing through content. In essence, we're referring to content that we give away freely, which people can consume without us asking for absolutely anything in return.

When you visit most malls in the U.S., sooner or later, you'll walk in front of the tea champion Teavana. When you do, you'll notice between two and four huge jugs of tea in front of their stores. You can just grab one of the small plastic cups from the side and serve yourself to try the tea they have available. Nobody asks you to pay, nor do you even have to talk to anyone. You can experience their tea right before you buy.

Another great example is the Red Bull YouTube channel. You will hardly ever find them talking directly about their products in those videos. They show action shots of bikes flying through the air and hang gliders leaping off of dangerous cliffs. They sell the values of the product — excitement and being awake to life — through this type of high-energy action-driven content.

This is the same approach we take toward our Gifts. It's all about giving people an experience of what we're all about, without any friction or requiring anything in exchange. Free videos, articles, guest posts, all of these are different forms of Gifts.

When building authority, most people focus exclusively on social media actions, but guess what? Social media is also a Gift. You're freely giving away the opportunity to interact with you. Yet many people think social media is all they need to focus on to raise their profile. When you focus your brand-building strategy exclusively on only ⅓ of a system, it is obviously going to be incomplete. Gifts are merely the beginning of people's journey when getting to know you and as you raise your authority in their eyes.

Checklist for Successful Gifts

☐ As its name suggests, a Gift **must** be free.

☐ It must require zero commitment from your customers.

☐ It indoctrinates about the values that your brand represents.

☐ It solves a real problem or desire that your target audience has.

THE MAGNET

Objectives

- Gives our potential clients even more opportunities to try the value that we offer.

- Solves a problem in a simple manner.

- Increases our appeal in our potential client's eyes.

- Expands the knowledge of our personal brand.

- Opens a channel to continue contacting this potential client.

After people consume Gifts, it's fine to present them with more value without requiring a monetary transaction, but through the Magnet we'll be asking for commitment from their end. Keep in mind, it isn't a prohibitive type of commitment we're talking about here. All we're asking for is some kind of contact information — email address, physical address, phone number, or anything else — in exchange for our valuable information.

You've probably seen retailers like JCPenney that offer 25%-50% discount coupons, but only if people sign up to their email newsletter.

Once they do sign up, they not only receive the discount, but they are also presented with all sorts of offers and exclusive deals on a frequent basis.

Have you ever signed up to receive an IKEA magazine? Yeah, you know it's not really a magazine…but it's so well laid out with great photography and ideas that it feels like one. Yet, to receive it at home — 100% for free — you first need to provide your home address along with other personal information. Oh, and they also have a digital version of their magaz… I mean, their catalog, which you can get by providing your email address.

In the same manner, we can develop content products that people will gladly give up their contact information to receive.

One of the Magnets we use at our firm is webinars. It can be either a live or pre-recorded session, where people can sign up, receive an invitation link, and watch one of our team members present on a variety of topics. It's distinct from my paid workshops, because it's completely free! All it requires is a quick sign up, and you can watch it right from home.

Some products that work as Magnets are: Webinars, apps, tools, ebooks, checklists, manuals, and many others.

Checklist for successful Magnets

☐ It must be free.

☐ You must have a database or some system to collect people's contact information.

☐ The perceived value of the Magnet must be ten times higher than the effort to provide the contact info.

☐ The Magnet must be a logical follow up to the Gifts, and should flow seamlessly into the next steps in our Product Staircase.

THE VELVET ROPE

Objectives

- Provides an irresistibly attractive offer.

- Separates buyers from non-buyers.

- Begins a pattern of purchasing from you.

- Eliminates your traffic costs.*

The Velvet Rope is a content product that has pretty much the same attraction qualities of the Gift and the Magnet, yet is entirely different because it is offered in exchange for a monetary transaction. However, its price is so ridiculously low that it is impossible to say no — as long as you are interested in the information offered.

Do you remember those Columbia House deals where they would give you 13 music cassettes or CDs for just 99¢? This is a classic example of a Velvet Rope. If you were a music lover, there was simply no way you could refuse this offer.

As you can see, the Velvet Rope separates buyers from non-buyers. Those who are able to resist this type of offer are typically people who would never be interested in investing in your services anyway. Provided your Velvet Rope is aligned with your value proposition, those who do purchase will be demonstrating two very important behaviors of a valuable audience member:

1. They will be interested in your subject of expertise.

2. They will be willing to pay — with real money — in exchange for something truly valuable.

Here's an example of one of the Velvet Ropes we offer at our firm. Often times, companies come to us with a problem around how their newly launched website is not being indexed in major search engines, such as Google or Bing. In response to this, we developed a 10-point checkup along with a list of fixes, which we call "Website Health Restoration." We offer this service for a very low price, which is a fraction of what we would charge to perform some serious re-builds on a site.

Clients that come in through this product not only receive a great service for an irresistibly attractive and economical price point, but they also receive a sense of the care and attention we offer to all of our clients. We have had many of them stay on with us for many years, happily paying for on diverse services.

Eliminating your advertising costs through a Velvet Rope product is an advanced tactic I teach at my workshops, and it goes a bit beyond the topic of this book. If you want to learn how to gather a large audience with zero costs, please sign up for my next free workshop here: http://cstps.co/velvetropewebinar

Checklist for a successful Velvet Rope

☐ It is offered for a ridiculously low price (it *must* have a monetary price).

☐ It needs to be tightly related to your main offer; in other words, only people interested in your main offer would be attracted to the Velvet Rope.

☐ It needs to be an offer that is too good to think about twice or to pass up.

THE HEART

Objectives

- Is connected to the main means of monetization for your business

- Shows up as supplemental material to your "Core offer" or "Main offer"

- Provides value to those who engage in business with you

Some types of businesses might already be based on delivering content, such as the case of an advisor, a coach, or an analyst. In many of these cases, information is the main deliverable, and therefore should be packaged as a valuable product that satisfies a particular need.

Even in the cases where the core business is comprised of much more than just information — such as services or products — it is a good idea to package valuable content alongside your deliverables. For example, if your process typically consists of a number of steps, you may be able to send over an infographic after each step is concluded, displaying the full process with an arrow pointing towards which step you and your clients are at.

If there is a specific task we need our clients to perform at a certain point in our process, instead of sending a long, boring email that they have to read, interpret, and then follow, you can send them a tutorial video with your own voice explaining step by step how to do it, while they follow your cursor on screen. This way, they can watch it on their own time, rewind and pause as they wish, and even delegate the task by sending our link to the video to one of their team members.

The Heart content product is a great way to inject additional perceived value to your service, especially if these services are ongoing. When on top of what you're supposed to deliver, you send along information that helps your clients become better informed — and as a side-benefit, helps increase your authority, which in turn confirms that they made the right choice by hiring you — it will make them feel like they're getting 120% of the value for their investment.

Checklist for a successful Heart

☐ It should help your clients become informed and satisfied in their decision to hire you.

☐ It should be related to your core offering.

☐ It should increase the perceived value of the product or service you were hired to deliver.

THE MULTIPLIER

Objectives

• Expand your core offering by increasing its utility or perceived value even further.

- Open opportunities to enhance your client's investment.

- Increase your lifetime customer value by selling even more services.

People normally refer to selling to existing clients as "upselling". This term might have a negative connotation, as nobody wants to be sold to. However, everyone who hires a service wants to feel like they've made a wise decision, and the Multiplier achieves this by expanding the impact that their initial investment has had on their business or their life.

Just as the Gift offers value ahead of the monetary transaction and the Heart expands the perceived value after the sale, the Multiplier offers value before and after considering other services you might offer to your existing clients. It entices clients to consider investing more with you, and also increases the perceived value of the services you are already providing.

At our firm, most of what we offer are done-for-you marketing services. However, our best clients are those who are equipped and informed to make wise marketing decisions. We offer half-day or full-day workshops at their own facilities, so that their staff is equipped to understand and even implement some of the marketing tactics that we recommend.

This workshop is not free, nor is it offered as a deliverable in our done-for-you packages. Clients who really want to upgrade their team's marketing skills are usually very excited to have us over as we spend a good amount of time with them, bringing reading materials, workshop booklets, and other Multiplier products.

Along the same line of thinking, some of your clients might be interested in recurring services after their first engagement with you, such as a maintenance or support retainer. Your Multiplier could be helpful content that sells the value of your additional services before ordering them, as well as content that informs your clients how to make the best of this additional investment with you.

The key to the Multiplier is that you need to have additional offers in the first place! The Multiplier will help close people on purchasing them, but these additional offers must have a defined set of deliverables and a specific price, so make sure to work on this first.

Checklist for a successful Multiplier

☐ Relates to additional services sold to existing clients.

☐ Can either entice clients to inquire about your additional services, or enhance the perceived value of your core offering.

☐ Is not shared with the "outside world," only with your clients.

CLIMBING THE PRODUCT STAIRCASE

As you've seen, this content framework goes well beyond the typical idea about content *only* being useful to attract new prospects. In this framework, we've seen how valuable content can also:

• Help identify new leads that would be interested in your services.

• Separate passive individuals from actual potential buyers of your offer.

• Enhance the perceived value of your core offering.

• Increase your bottom line by leading towards additional offers for your existing clients.

You will notice that there is a common thread in all of these possibilities: in all forms of content, you are still solving problems and satisfying needs well in advance of deeper and more extended business engagements with you. This generates affinity and trust in people who may be thrilled to hire your services, which is a fantastic expectation to generate.

Content Touchpoints

By now, you understand that you must share value in advance of any monetary transaction with your prospective clients. As we've said before, people simply will not hire your services if they don't first get a taste of the value that you can bring to them.

A huge potential pitfall with this approach is the "build it and they will come" notion that was popularized in the film Field of Dreams, yet has nothing to do with us as professionals. The fact that you are developing valuable content is all fine and well; but if nobody is consuming it, what good is it?

Although I won't go deeply into content distribution — it would be repetitive, as I've already done this in my other books — let's discuss three touchpoints where your audience may come into contact with your content. This will help you gain a wider perspective of the different options you have when reaching people who may want to do business with you.

ONLINE CONTENT

In this exciting era of everything-digital, this is the first type of touchpoint that people typically think of when they consider producing content. There are many types of digital media and distribution channels that can allow you to demonstrate your grasp on your professional topics.

The Web is probably the medium that will help you make your ideas available to your audience with the least amount of friction and blockage. Pretty much everyone these days has a web-enabled device in our pockets, so your content can be made available to the world with just a few taps.

Some of the types of online content I currently use to share valuable ideas are blog posts, articles, infographics, social media posts, live videos, ephemeral stories (think Snapchat or Facebook Stories), and podcasts, among a few others. As you can tell, I am a content-generating freak, as it is what we at our firm do best, but I am in no way suggesting that you need to do as much as I currently do. Just pick one or two forms of content and keep outputting your ideas consistently.

OFFLINE CONTENT

Valuable and unique content doesn't have to be limited to online sharing. Your audience may appreciate receiving your ideas through physical media, like a printed and mailed newsletter, a magazine, or even a non-salesy letter or brochure.

We've even produced brochures that have integrated HD screens in them, and when the recipient opens it up, a lively video presentation plays. You get digital video played through a non web-enabled device, and it's quite effective. Depending on your video content, you can make it feel just one step away from being face-to-face in front of the person receiving it.

IN-PERSON CONTENT

The third content touchpoint I'll discuss is the type you deliver while being physically present in front of one or more members of your target audience.

The most wide-reaching form of in-person content is usually delivered when you speak in front of an audience, whether at a conference, workshop or some other event. Examples of this can be informational handouts, workbooks, or even thumb-drives with additional content.

You might want to prepare content for your more intimate settings as well, like a presentation or workshop for a small group. I've made many lasting business connections that have begun through a valuable corporate training session.

You can even prepare content for one-on-one sessions with prospects and clients. In fact, I've noticed that when people realize that a meeting with you has structure — meaning that it has a middle, a beginning, and an end, and that there is a clear point to the meeting—they are more likely to walk away feeling like their time was well spent. A way to impress this feeling of structure is by following along a brochure or worksheet that spells out the sections of your meeting.

Are You In Business?

In this section, I've given you a tour around different ways to align the extensions of your personal brand with your true business value. It's the only way to ensure that the time and energy you spend actually helps advance your professional endeavors forward.

At the beginning of this book, we established that attention is the most valuable currency of our day. By this point, you have learned about many different tools to take firm action towards representing your business value, without wavering or becoming distracted.

> "In response to my petty excuses, he firmly said, 'Buddy, you're either in business, or you're not'."

One of the most profound bits of business advice I have ever heard was given to me during a mentoring session. I had been coming up with all kinds of excuses for not taking the action that the mentor was recommending. In response to my petty excuses, he firmly said, "Buddy, you're either in business, or you're not."

Think about it for a second. How many times have we gotten distracted with stuff that entertains us and have failed to follow a consistent path that will make us more credible for what we do in business? Many of us are just wasting people's valuable attention, yammering on about sports, politics, and the latest episode of a TV show, while people listening to us don't really understand what we do, and therefore are never able to seek our help nor connect us with a friend who could use our services.

Most people build up countless reasons why it's bad to be "all about business," or some other caricature they've drawn up against the idea of having strong Alignment between their brand and their business purpose.

Whether you're in the group that is rolling their sleeves and ready to take on these tasks, or the group that's content with their excuses, listen once again to the advice given to me: *"You're either in business, or you're not."*

You are either always in an attitude where you are eager and hungry to portray yourself as the most qualified person to help others, or you are just doing what you do as a hobby, and are more interested in taking the easy ride, fooling around, laying back, and staying entertained along with the masses.

If you *are* in business, keep reading. I think you'll love the next chapter, where we'll talk about how to be unique and stand out.

CHAPTER 9

Awesomeness: Standing Out

Excellence is rare. Those who embrace it are guaranteed to shine.

The Painful Truth About You

L et's begin this chapter with a serious truth about you. Although it might utterly offend you, make you want to hate me, or even close the book and walk away, we have to acknowledge this truth before moving on. I'm very aware of the risks involved in telling this to you, yet it would not help one bit if I allowed you to walk away believing an absolute lie.

Countless others, people who love you dearly and want only the best for you, have the habit of telling you the exact opposite of what I'm about to tell you. I'm about to become that jerk who disagrees with your sweet momma or your loving partner, but so be it.

Here's the deal: when it comes to business, *you are not as special as you think you are*. There are thousands of other people who can offer the exact same services that you offer, at the exact same price — or even lower — by following practically the same process, and with a very similar set of outcomes.

You haven't closed the book? Still with me? Okay, good.

The reason I want to break down any delusions you might have about being unique and incredibly special is because I actually want to build you back up to be *unique and incredibly special* — only in a realistic manner. I don't want you to be blind-sided upon suddenly realizing that in your profession you are a speck of sand among a beach of similar options… like I once was.

You see, when I started my business, I could have sworn that people would be impressed when I just showed them what I could do. I failed to realize there were competitors racing for a nibble of the same exact pie wherever I showed up, and that I was talking exactly like each and every one of them. Every time I talked about my profession, people listening to me already had someone in mind that they had met previously, whom they automatically compared me to.

When I realized this, I felt dejected and even a bit depressed. I felt like I had stupidly chosen the wrong line of business. I had chosen to be a guitar enthusiast at a crowded music school. I was as unique as a tattooed guy at a biker's conference.

When I was able to lift my head and look beyond myself, I realized that I wasn't the only one feeling this way. In fact, most every professional that was out in the market felt somewhat like this, regardless of which profession they were in. It's not that I had chosen the wrong profession, because from where I could see, everyone in business suffered the same difficulties and had to wade against as much competition. Everyone needed to stand out.

It wasn't until I internalized the fact that I wasn't as special as I thought I was, that I was clear-headed enough to look deep within myself, my skillset, my take on the market, to find what *really* made me special.

What makes you special isn't the profession you've chosen, the title you throw after stating your name, the fact that you have a business card, the products or services you sell, absolutely none of that.

What Makes You Special

The aspect that will make you stand out in a crowded market has nothing to do with the obvious things you might think about first. You know the difference between attempting to sell by presenting a ton of qualities and features—which anyone can do—versus showing someone the emotional benefits of selecting your option. The emotional, intangible appeal of things wins every time.

What makes you special is a quality I call "Awesomeness." It's quite unfortunate that the word "awesome" has become synonymous with "Okay" or "pretty good" in our day. "We're meeting for coffee on Monday, awesome." I'm as guilty of this as anyone, as I misuse this word all the time.

What I mean here when I say "Awesomeness" is what it used to mean since the word began its use in the English language. Awe is defined as, "a feeling of reverential respect mixed with fear or wonder." It's what you feel when you are in the presence of something that makes your jaw just drop. You feel it right in the middle of your gut when you see or hear something that is just so outstanding that at that moment you know you're in the presence of something you won't find every day.

The one secret to stand out among your crowded space is to be awesome, inducing a sense of amazement because you have managed to do what you do with a level of passion and excellence that just seems so elusive to everyone else in your space.

You need to dare to do things differently. Zag when they zig. Dance when they sprint. Sing when they scream. Do things more differently and artfully than everyone else, and you'll win.

Setting The Standard

No matter which industry you operate within, the standard has already been set for you. It could have been set by many others who came before you and operated a certain way, or through rules and regulations that seem to restrict everyone to a certain set of guidelines, or by market trends that have favored those who lean a certain way.

I believe it's possible to not only set a standard above the status quo, but to actually *become* the new standard. How do I know this? Because even in the toughest and most crowded of industries, I *constantly* find people who manage stand out and become the reference point for everyone after them. They haven't found the end of the rainbow or stumbled upon a magic horseshoe; all they've managed to do is become the reference point through everything they do.

During a season of our business, we spoke to a large number of financial planners, as we were performing research on a potential product for them. I asked how they managed to promote themselves, and all of them — without a single exception — gave me the exact same story: "My industry is so regulated, I can't really do much to promote myself." Since then, I've spoken to real estate agents, mortgage brokers, attorneys, and guess what? They all seem to tell the *exact* same story.

Yet, in all of these industries, I still see examples of professionals who, despite "playing by the rules" and keeping within any existing regulations, have managed to always be awesome and shine above the masses walking on paths others have treaded for them.

It takes a certain kind of boldness to not only excel above any given standard, but to actually be so daring as to *become* a new standard. I know you have it in you. You wouldn't have read this far if you weren't willing to consider taking on a different perspective.

The Relentless Pursuit

Always being awesome isn't something you'll be able to achieve overnight. It takes hard work, a strong level of commitment, and massive dedication. It requires a high level of disgust against the thought of settling with the status quo.

As soon as you step out and claim being awesome as your new mission, you will confront numerous forces that will try to woo you back into walking in line. It's much easier. It's less stressful. It's what you're supposed to do. They say you can spot the pioneers because they have arrows stuck on their backs.

To this I say: Who cares! Isn't it all worth it? The other option is to be just another puppy at the bottom of the table nibbling away at the crumbs. You have only a limited number of years remaining in your profession. Is doing just what others do the vision you have for your career? Why not see yourself taking on greater challenges — along with the greater rewards for overcoming them?

If you're open to this, then the only option you have is to make being awesome your persistent mission.

The irony around taking on this mission is that you will never achieve the ultimate state of being awesome. It's not an end goal, but rather an endless process. Everything can be improved, so there is always work to do. What will make you stand out isn't a status level you've managed to arrive at, but rather an ambition you've switched on that burns deep within your being: you have decided to pursue awesomeness for the rest of your life.

> "Everything can be improved, so there is always work to do."

This is one trait that people notice from afar when you *don't* have it, but might not be able to point out when you do have it. In other words, when you're not in the mindset of achieving excellence in everything you do, you're subconsciously labeled as "just another attorney," or "just another business coach," or "just another _____" (fill in the blank with your profession). On the other hand, people can sense from far away when you're one of those rare folks who are uncomfortable about being just like everyone else. They will *feel* there is something different about you.

And who do you think people desire to do business with? The ones you can find any day at the local meetup or networking event? Or someone who embodies awesomeness to such a degree that people absolutely know they are in the presence of a one-of-a-kind specialist in their space?

Awesomeness Requires Persistence

T he quality we're talking about here will help separate you from the others in your space, but as I said, it's not simple nor is it easy to achieve. Have you ever heard the phrase, "If it were easy, everyone would be doing it"?

The reason awesomeness makes you stand out in business is *precisely* because not everyone has the grit to be awesome. It's much easier to do whatever others are already doing. In the wilderness of business, it takes less effort to walk along pastures which others have already flattened, rather than swing your machete and chop away at the tall blades of grass.

> "The reason awesomeness makes you stand out in business is precisely because not everyone has the grit to be awesome."

Yet, the brave ones swinging their machetes are the ones who command respect. They are the first ones people think about when wondering who to refer business to and also the ones entitled to charge more for their services.

This level of grit is an attitude you install, not a club you sign up for. It flows from deep within your will, and it manifests through bruises and hard effort even at times when there is no reward in sight.

You can no longer be impressed with the norm, and at times this can be extremely painful. Your standards need to be lifted so high that even your own work begins to look deficient. Most people can't take this strong blow to their egos, and give up as soon as they feel the slightest sting. They can't let go of the illusion that everything they do — no matter how little effort they put behind it — deserves a slow clap and a consolation prize. It's hard to swallow the fact that everything can be improved, and therefore, perfection is strived for, but never fully reached.

If you do decide to pursue this race towards being awesome, you need to know that it takes place on a very long track without a finish line. What will lift you high above everyone else in your space isn't the fact that you won the medal. It's that you *decided* to run rather than stroll along on the slow lane.

It took me so much time to understand this. For far too long, I thought that "competition" in business meant a race to become the best, but many years have passed since I stopped thinking this way. I realized that the real competition is between those who decide to be awesome versus everyone else.

Here's an even more surprising fact: People who pursue awesomeness are actually way more collaborative and helpful to each other — i.e. non-competitive — than the ones living in the herd, who are constantly battling each other for scraps. Those of us who strive to go above and beyond the norm are constantly referring business to each other, and the reason for this is quite logical. If you're working on developing a brand that is unique and outstanding, you'll even want other professionals you recommend to have the same standards that you strive towards in everything else. It makes zero sense to send business to someone you're not impressed with.

You need to begin running the race, fighting the battle, raising the banner that shows that you're on a journey that is way more significant than just getting by in life and business.

How Awesomeness Puts More Money In Your Pocket

S ome of you might think that what I'm talking about here is just a "good-to-have," but that it has very little to do with actually getting busy and doing business. I couldn't disagree more. What I'm discussing here is a key towards growing your business, and generating more revenue.

There are four distinct ways in which following this advice to always be awesome will make you more money:

1- It Makes Your Solution More Desirable

How do high-end brands like Bulova, Apple, and Maserati manage to make people crave for their products? They simply maintain a standard of quality that communicates that their offer cannot found easily anywhere else.

You can achieve this desirability when your personal brand communicates awesomeness. In order to have more opportunities than you could possibly serve, you first need to show that what you offer actually has the rare qualities that every other regular solution could only dream about having.

2- It Commands Attention

When your personal brand is able to impress, it is also worthy of more Transactions of Attention. People are happy to invest their focus on worthwhile experiences. When more people pay attention, you are able to offer even more experiences with your brand along with the value you can bring, which will translate into more business for you.

> "Awesomeness is almost impossible to ignore."

Awesomeness is almost impossible to ignore. It's in such rare supply, that people feel that passing it up is not an option.

3- It Sets A High-End Expectation

If you've already set a higher standard — rather, if you have already *become* the higher standard, you will have built a clear path towards charging whatever you want. Your ideal client will feel fine about paying a high-end rate for a high-end service, but a high-end service is always preceded by a high-end expectation.

On the other hand, don't even think about raising your rates or offering more high-end services if you haven't yet managed to communicate awesomeness in everything you do. It simply won't fly.

From the very beginning, you must show that your service follows a different standard than the rest of the pack, which is how you can be confident about commanding a fee at the top of the table.

4- It Eases The Sale

I've had prospects fire agencies that are ten times larger than our firm, just to do business with us. Whereas those larger agencies have to bring in large teams for a well-rehearsed presentation, sometimes I just show up alone for coffee or lunch and walk away with a signed contract.

How is this possible? It certainly isn't because we're cheaper. It has everything to do with the fact that we can show that our approach responds to a much higher standard than those guys. While those big agencies are just looking to churn their clients through their "machine," from the very first meeting we show that by working with us, our focus, care, and attention will be on *them*. People in business aren't used to being treated with such attention by their service providers, so in a weird way the tables get turned and they end up *asking* about how they can do business with us.

Your desire towards being awesome needs to burn right through your veins. People on the other side of the negotiation table can sense this drive from where they're sitting. Any resistance they might have against doing business with you dissolves away, and in its place, a sincere wish to do business with you settles in its place.

Awesome Means Easy

Of course, I don't mean to suggest that it's easy to be awesome. I would be lying to you if I told you that all it takes to be awesome is getting out of bed, raising your fists to the sky, and screaming, "I'm awesome!" It requires much more than posting on social media that you're awesome. It takes hard work and a willingness to take risks that you will be severely uncomfortable about.

What I mean by "Awesome Means Easy" is that when prospects and clients sense that it is easy to work with you, you immediately earn awesome points. Amazon understands this. By rolling out their Amazon Prime program, in which subscribers pay no additional shipping charges and even get their order shipped in two days or less, they knew they would give their customers one less thing to think about, making their lives easier. I've even heard people say "I love my Amazon Prime" as if it were their best friend. So easy, it's awesome.

We've worked very hard to streamline our process to make things easier for our clients in similar manners. For example, by recording our initial kickoff meeting with our clients with a professional microphone, following a carefully designed interview script, we have eliminated numerous email exchanges bothering the client with questions about their business, or worse yet, asking them to *work for us* by filling in a creative brief. When we have a question, instead of annoying them, most of the time we just open the audio interview and the answer is usually right there.

So many professionals make their clients' lives difficult, particularly during the onboarding process. To become one of their clients, you need to meet 2-3 times, pick up their interruptive calls, wade through emails to find four different forms you need to sign and send back (even re-learn how to use a fax!) and other ridiculous gymnastics.

If you are being hired to solve a problem, you do not have permission to create new problems for your client. It's reasonable that you may have certain requirements to kick off each stage of the project, but why not ask for most of the requirements up front? It's reasonable to expect feedback and approval before moving forward at certain points, but is sending this feedback as easy as possible for them?

If making it easy for your client means a bit more time and resources spent on your end, it's still worth it. Your client will be much happier, you will have a client for a longer period, and they will rave with their peers about how delightful it is to work with you. What they subconsciously have in the back of their mind is that:

a) **"You get it"**: You have such a grasp on what you do, that you're not taxing the client with unnecessary questions. You can see the end goal, and demonstrate that you know how to get them there.

b) **"We have a great experience working with you"**: You never have the look of anxiety whenever you are presented with a difficult obstacle, which would only stress them out more. Rather, you're in control of the process, with helpful answers and insights along the way.

c) **"You're easy to work with"**: You proactively take care of unexpected issues that pop up along the way, and let them know after they've been resolved.

This last point is key for this "Awesome Means Easy" idea. Those unexpected goodies that come along the way during your service will make you shine. I'm talking about much more than a Christmas card or a box of chocolates you mail out. Here are some examples of these "goodies":

- You found a problem and solved it for them without even asking them if it would be okay to do so.

- You found a way to reduce <u>your own fee,</u> yet continue offering the same services in your agreement.

- You gave them an additional convenience without even asking them or charging anything extra, just because you thought it was the right thing to do.

- Instead of requiring them to read a 4-page PDF to learn how to do something, you recorded a personalized 1-minute video and sent it to them, saving them 15 minutes or more of their time.

- You agreed to meet with another service provider who works with them, just to save them from uncomfortably passing along technical information that was out of their specialty and because you knew it would help avoid further problems down the line.

These tips have to do with your current clients, and when you do these things consistently, your prospects can also sense that it is easy to work with you. You simply "have it together."

Nobody wants to hire someone who will create more work or anxiety for them. In the very first meeting, if you are able to show the outcome they can expect, the pitfalls along the way that you take care of, and the exact process you have designed and implemented with your existing clients, people have no option but to be impressed at your awesomeness and therefore will want that level of ease in their lives or their businesses as well.

Awesomeness Demands Quality

Another aspect that immediately points out that someone is awesome is that they are dripping with a passion for high quality. Every element that represents their brand demonstrates care and attention to detail, both on the visual end as well as in clarity of communication.

Every single day, I see professionals putting together a list of items they must have, like business cards, website, etc. and then fishing for the cheapest alternative just to get it off their plate and move on. Recently, someone I know told me that their cheaply made website was the cause for them losing three potential clients.

You may not want to spend time or money into your business assets, but let me be very clear that you are always selling the quality of your services, whether you want to or not.

I realize that everyone might not have the advantage of a critical eye around quality. Some people are just process oriented and have been trained to focus entirely on the function of things and never on their form. When developing their brand, or hiring someone to help them do so, they lack the ability to determine whether they're putting out their best impression or not.

Here are two techniques that I picked up in art school that can be applied toward evaluating the aesthetic quality of anything you might come across. When you learn to apply these techniques, you will be better equipped to put them to use when looking at everything related to your own brand.

Formal Analysis

The first one has to do with being able to describe what is right in front of you in terms that are as specific as possible. There is so much that takes place around you, but your mind usually just processes the essentials — just the functional aspects — and then discards the form of things.

This habit to ignore form deceives you when, for example, you are having your business card designed and you focus only on whether your name is misspelled or not. So you approve the design, without even realizing that your name is printed in red font over a blue background, and will be impossible to read by most human beings. Furthermore, you weren't prepared to stop and consider whether those colors were the most appropriate ones to communicate what you want to portray through your brand. Had you practiced formal analysis, you would have been able to catch this right away.

Here's an exercise to learn how to perform a Formal Analysis, which should take you no more than 5-10 minutes:

1. Find a visual piece you want to practice on, which is **not** your own. Look for a business card, a brochure, a magazine ad, anything that falls under the category of "marketing materials."

2. Hold it up and begin to describe its aspects — it can be in your head, or you can say it out loud — as if you had a visually impaired person in front of you and wanted them to understand how it looks. Describe the shape of the piece, the colors of the page, the colors of the background, how many different fonts it has, how many different sizes of fonts appear on the page.

3. Also pay attention to any photos or icons you might find. If it has photos of people, describe the person, what they're wearing,

whether they're wearing a ring on one of their fingers. Every little detail counts.

4. Resist the urge to talk about the *function* of the piece, or about your opinion of the piece.

5. Once you're done listing every perceivable aspect of the piece, go one step further. Is there anything you haven't described yet? Go for even the most ridiculously small and obvious details. Don't leave anything up to assumptions.

6. When you're done describing every single detail, close your eyes and visualize the piece you've just described. Can you see the piece in your mind, with all of its details? Picture it in your head as clearly as possible.

7. Open your eyes and look again at the piece. Were there any differences between what you saw in your head and what you're now seeing in front of you?

8. Ask yourself: Why were there differences between what you visualized and what was right in front of you? Was it because you didn't pay attention to all of the details? Was it because your description of the details wasn't rich enough?

Your answer to the questions in step 8 will show the reasons why you might have had difficulty evaluating the quality of things you come into contact with. By noticing the habits in the way you currently think, you'll catch yourself making an effort against ignoring this the next time you need to judge whether something you produce is of a sufficient quality.

ICONOGRAPHIC ANALYSIS

In the previous exercise, we exclusively observed the *form* of things. Another way to analyze your surroundings is by questioning what each detail *means*. In other words, what these elements communicate without using linguistic resources (words, sentences, etc.).

Our natural tendency is to think that words are the only element that transmits meaning, so for this type of analysis you should purposely overlook the words on any piece you use. This exercise actually works much better when you perform it on pieces in a language you don't understand, which will allow you to focus on the nonverbal components; but even if you have a piece in a language you do know, the goal here is to avoid paying attention to what the words mean.

For this type of analysis, we need to analyze what each non-linguistic element communicates, and more importantly, if what each piece communicates is in line with the brand and functional goals of our piece.

One of the most frequent errors I see happens when a consultative professional puts forth a piece to communicate their business proposition, and although they intend to be taken seriously, their piece has a color palette inspired by the wallpaper in a candy store, and uses a font that would make Comic Sans laugh. No matter how serious the words are, the piece as a whole reflects another message entirely. The iconography's light-hearted approach to their prospects' problems unfortunately gets them nowhere to convince others to invest in their serious solution.

This problem usually stems precisely from not exercising our ability to go beyond the written word, and ask what every little detail communicates.

We recently reviewed an online presence an executive transportation service company. Their site was well put together and communicated their value, except for the fact that they had insisted that there be a shaky high-speed first-person video driving down the highway. Until we alerted them, they never stopped to consider that a high-speed video could communicate reckless driving over the speed limit.

Learning to analyze your brand iconographically is essential to reach the level of excellence we've been discussing in this chapter.

The integrity of your message depends on how much each little bit supports your tone, your message, and what your prospects wish to hear.

DOES IT LOOK LIKE AN ERROR?

"If it looks like a duck, swims like a duck, and quacks like a duck, then it's probably a duck!" In like manner, if it looks like an error, it probably will be interpreted as one...even if it really isn't an error.

This question "Does it look like an error?" has saved me a ton of shame when performing quality control on my brand assets. Something I'm about to put out might be exactly to my liking, but may seem like an error when viewing it from the perspective of someone just encountering my brand for the very first time.

If it *can* be perceived as an error, you better believe that it *will* be perceived as one. In the least significant of cases, people might think you are careless with your brand, and may interpret that you are as careless with the work you perform for your clients. In the worst of cases, the perceived error just might absorb all of people's attention, and your message will never get a chance to cut through.

A few situations that can fool people into thinking there is an error include:

- Elements on a page with a bit too much or too little space in between them.

- Items that aren't centered, but feel like they should be.

- Sentences that are there just to fill in the space.

- An image that overlaps the essential features of another.

- An object that feels like it's barely visible, yet visible enough to distract.

- A voice inflection that feels random and not in line with the meaning of the words spoken.

When something feels like an error, it's better to modify or just eliminate it, rather than deal with the perception of coming across as clumsy.

The Clarity Test

When you're working on your message, one of the most common situations you will encounter is that you're so close to your craft, everything makes sense only to yourself and nobody else. It's natural to make assumptions as you develop your content, but you must always remember that business growth is about reaching people who have never heard from you; therefore, others might be unaware about a boatload of context that you might be taking for granted.

This includes anything from opinions, methodologies, and even what we normally call "inside jokes" — which are often so *inside* that the outside world is left scratching their head wondering what it really means!

Unfortunately, unclear messages scream mediocrity. Even a baboon can express itself unclearly. On the other hand, clarity is a signal of brilliance.

Clarity also shows empathy. If you cared just about yourself, you wouldn't be concerned about your message being clear. The mere fact that you're crafting a clear message shows that you care about others.

The easiest way to check whether your message is clear is to ask someone else outside of your immediate team. Tell them to read or listen to the brand piece you're developing, and ask them to let you know whether they feel like they understand what you're trying to say. If for any reason they do not understand it, then ask them what particular bits might have confused them.

Quite frankly, although I think getting other people's feedback is absolutely fine, I think it's best to not rely entirely on outside support to perform a simple clarity check. It's more cumbersome to depend on other people's time to give you feedback. More importantly, I think it's healthy to train yourself to be able to find out whether you are expressing yourself clearly or not.

One way to do this is to take a 24-hour break—or longer if possible—from the piece you're developing. Then come back to it imagining that you are someone else. Just imagine you are someone who is coming to know you for the very first time through your presentation.

Would a first look leave a clear impression in someone else's mind about the message you wish to communicate? If anything is concerning or makes you feel insecure, it's probably because it still needs work.

I've performed this exact clarity test on the words you are reading right now. I came back to read them a few weeks after I originally wrote them and tweaked many of the words because I didn't feel like they communicated what I wanted. Anything that might have given the impression that I wasn't thinking clearly, I rewrote or even took out.

Final Thoughts About Awesomeness

I n this chapter, we've looked at tips to show that your service is awesome, well before you send your first invoice or charge your first fee, by just ensuring that every aspect of your brand is above the standard in your field.

By applying these tips, you will immediately stand out from the crowd and competition will become the least of your concerns.

But what happens after the sale? Does your personal brand still matter after you close a new client?

CHAPTER 10

Sell You *Beyond* The Sale

Beyond The Sale?

S o far, everything we've talked about has been around creating the strongest impression before any discussion around monetary transactions takes place to attract more opportunities and close more sales. However, the same principles apply towards increasing and maintaining business beyond the initial sale.

So much of sales and marketing is exclusively focused on top-line tactics, yet in most business fields, acquiring a customer is merely the beginning. It makes very little sense to close tens or even hundreds of new clients, just so they end up dissatisfied, while you fall out of grace in their eyes.

It costs up to 5 times more effort and resources to acquire a new client than it takes to maintain an existing business relationship[9]. Knowing and applying the tips I've shared in this book will make attracting new business much easier than if you didn't take action on them.

However, if you also want to extend these initial engagements into long-lasting business relationships, you would benefit from continuing the expectation your brand generates well beyond the initial closing. After all, if you've managed to sell yourself as a reliable resource to solve their problems, why wouldn't they engage again with you?

---

9 "Five Customer Retention Tips for Entrepreneurs," by Alex Lawrence; www.forbes.com/sites/alexlawrence/2012/11/01/five-customer-retention-tips-for-entrepreneurs/#72f2d4da5e8d

Just as you've elevated and clarified your profile to attract new business, the same tactics are also useful to:

a) **Retain clients** and maintain a solid and fruitful business relationship with them.

b) **Increase revenue per client** by opening new opportunities to increase your business with them.

c) **Get more referrals** by motivating them to refer you to contacts who might also be looking for your services.

What Will Happen If You Skip This Chapter

S ome side effects may occur, including burning skin, insomnia, discomfort, mild headaches, dizziness, nausea, itchy skin and uncontrollable bowel movements.

Okay…those things might not happen, but it would still be really awful if you stopped reading here. Here's how I know:

Before I applied these tips, I used be in contact with many, many different clients each month, with whom I closed very small deals. They were just looking for quick fixes, not the deep, transformative processes I now offer. As a result, we would finish the small transaction, and I would never hear from them again.

To make matters worse, each of these new contacts generated very little revenue for the company, so I was in a constant uphill battle to grow my contact list and close small deals just to get by.

I take full responsibility for this flaw, as I completely failed to position myself as someone who could solve people's deeper issues. Even if these people were willing to pay more for a full solution, they would never pay *me*, because I never pitched myself as a valuable provider of these solutions. By starting at the bottom, I inadvertently pitched myself as the exact opposite — a non-valuable independent contractor!

Let me use a musician's analogy that I learned from my first piano teacher:

If I could smoothly play Liszt's Hungarian Rhapsody No. 02, you would immediately assume that I can also play a much simpler tune like "Twinkle, Twinkle, Little Star." However, if all I'm able to show is that I can play "Twinkle, Twinkle, Little Star," you would have zero grounds to assume that I can play even the first two or three bars of Liszt's masterpiece. In fact, it would be quite reasonable to assume that I *can't* play it, as it would be well above the level demonstrated.

This is very similar to what was happening to me. Even though I had the experience and skills to help solve my clients' deeper issues, my personal brand was non-existent, and I showed up as someone who could only solve the "Twinkle, Twinkle Little Star" problems that nobody would want to pay any significant amount of money to address. When these clients needed deeper, more meaningful help, they would reasonably ignore me and seek out help from someone else.

In the following pages, you will discover how I changed my approach and actions, and now enjoy happier, more fruitful business relationships.

Will You Be A Trusted Advisor?

When you come into any business relationship, there are two extreme attitudes that you should be careful about avoiding. Either of these will de-value your contribution in the relationship, as well as what your brand is worth.

a) **Telling only what you want to say.** By this, I mean that your advice is only focused on the benefit you can get out of the relationship with this client.

b) **Telling only what the client wants to hear.** This means that you keep quiet about your sincere opinions and give them exactly what they are asking for, even if you realize that it's not what's best for them.

Either of these attitudes position you as useless to their purposes. The first one shows that you are not invested in their success, whereas the second one makes you entirely disposable and unnecessary.

The proper attitude is to give exactly the advice that needs to be given, regardless of whether it benefits you in the end, or whether it's what the other person doesn't want to hear. Only this approach will turn you into the Trusted Advisor that they are really needing by their side.

This approach will require that you disagree with your clients now and then. I disagree constantly with my clients, and I make sure to express clearly when I don't agree with them, as well as why I feel that way. You should always make sure to disagree respectfully, but in the end your clients will be much happier when you express your sincere thoughts in a bold, unwavering manner.

> "Your clients will be much happier when you express your sincere thoughts in a bold, unwavering manner."

Think about it: They are actually paying you to point them in the right direction! If you deny them the right advice in response to their issues, you would be selling them a cheaper set of goods than what they are paying for.

From the beginning of the client relationship, you must think about yourself as a provider of valuable advice and act as one in every interaction you have with them.

Standing On The Same Step

Along with positioning yourself as a trusted advisor, it is very important to enter into business relationships with the understanding that you and your client are in equal professional standing and that as such, you deserve mutual respect.

So many professionals get hired, and immediately assume a submissive, "yes, sir" or "yes, ma'am" attitude. Every time I see this, my heart breaks a little.

They have studied hard, endured many grueling experiences to get to where they are, but now assume that they're their client's underlings just because they are getting paid to get a job done.

News Flash: Slavery is no longer cool!

Your most valuable and grateful clients won't be the ones who enjoy the satisfaction of being a boss to one more person. Your best clients will be the ones who are convinced that you are a capable individual who is adding valuable perspectives to their business operations.

Being treated as an underling actually places a heavier burden on your clients, as they need to invest more of their time and resources. They can never fully release control from the duties you are supposed to be taking care of, as trust in you is non-existent. In one instance, I had a client say to me, "I love coming to our consultation meetings because these are the only meetings in my schedule where ideas bounce both ways. Most of my team members expect **me** to come up with all the answers!"

Your clients don't hire you just to get a particular problem solved. They also crave peace of mind. They want to be absolutely certain that the main problem, as well as the side-effects of solving that main problem, will get taken care of. They want someone to alert them about hidden weak spots, and provide them with suggestions on how to avoid any potential issues in their future. They want to feel like they have the right person in charge.

This only happens if you consider yourself a business partner standing on the same step of the staircase, rather than an outsider looking upward from many steps below.

Yes, you are there to help them, but it doesn't help anyone if you fail to take a leadership attitude towards resolving the issue that got you hired in the first place.

Expanding Your Business

One of the benefits of having a fruitful and lasting business relationship with a client is that you'll be able to open opportunities to offer other services, beyond those you were originally hired for. If you position yourself as someone who can do something well and you actually fulfill what you proposed, you've gained enough credibility to take on other types of requests from the same client.

As we've seen, a brand is all about forming an expectation in others, but the health of that brand hangs on whether that expectation is fulfilled or not. By beginning with a solid personal brand well ahead of being hired, and also continuing this expectation throughout your engagement, you will manage to remain top of mind as someone who can take on other types of requests.

Here are four ways you can position yourself to generate more business from a single client:

UPSELLING

This term has earned a bad reputation, because it brings to mind sleazy salesmen pushing to squeeze every single nickel and dime out of their clients. This is absolutely not what I'm referring to here.

In situations in which the client's needs go beyond the initial scope of the agreement, it's quite reasonable to present them with a higher-ticket option that will satisfy their needs. You've been brought in to solve a problem, and failing to do so just because you were afraid to present a solution that required a greater investment will only end up disappointing the client.

CROSS-SELLING

This takes place when you offer additional services aside from those the client originally contracts you for. This is also a reasonable dynamic within a successful business relationship. Very often, the initial service you presented to the client won't be comprehensive enough to cover every single need that they might have. This is when it might make sense to hire you for other services that will also help them.

You should ensure that those additional services are also in alignment with your core specialty, and that you're able to deliver them with excellence. Otherwise, if you fail to deliver, you might risk spoiling the whole relationship. In other words, don't try to fulfill every need the client has just because they are willing to spend more money. It's perfectly fine to let them know that their request isn't what you do best, or to refer them to someone who can serve them better.

AFFILIATE PARTNERSHIPS

In many occasions in which a client has needs beyond the ones you can directly supply, you will have the chance to refer them to other resources and solution providers in your network of whom you trust. You may even receive a commission for this type of referral, but it's not always the case.

The most critical element is to ensure that you refer them to someone who you are absolutely certain will get the job done. To do this correctly, you need to vet and sometimes even hire these partners yourself first so you can be assured that they can fulfill what they promise.

This investment into research will be time well spent. When you refer your clients to a solid service provider, your brand's level of credibility will only increase further. You will show up not only as someone who can solve problems directly, but also a reliable gateway towards valuable solutions of other sorts. The strength of your network can become an appreciable aspect of your brand's value.

MOTIVATING REFERRALS

One of the clearest signs that your client is satisfied with your help occurs when they are happy to pass your name along to other contacts in their network. This shows that they appreciate your specialty so much that they are willing to connect you to people with whom they also appreciate. Your value becomes your client's gift to others.

Stats show that although 83% of consumers show willingness to introduce a referral after a positive experience, only 29% actually take a step forward and do so.[10] This suggests that more than half of your clients would be happy to refer you along, but something seems to be blocking them from doing so.

The one factor that often blocks clients from referring you to others is not having you at the top of their minds as a source of help for them. Every tip we've discussed so far in this book will help you stay within their sights, even after your client has hired you and has been working with you. By becoming consistently attractive, authentic, aligned, and awesome, they will organically come up with opportunities to connect you with their friends and business contacts. I've seen this happen time and time again.

Here are a few additional tips to follow to generate more referrals from your existing clients:

---

10 As seen in research from Texas Tech University.

Let them see your acquisition marketing. Without becoming annoying, it's okay to let them peek at what you're doing to get new clients. How else will they know that you have an opening, or a special offer?

Some of my friends are opposed and even fearful of their clients seeing their activity on social media, but I disagree that this is a problem. I want them to see how I am constantly positioning myself as a provider of solutions. When my clients see this, they may be able to remember someone in their network who recently vented about a particular problem.

On occasions when we've had events exclusively for new clients, I've sent the invitation to my clients in case they can think of someone who they consider should attend.

By letting them become aware of my activity to connect with more clients, they are reminded that we are open for business.

Provide an unexpected helpful resource. As you produce valuable content to establish your authority, one of your pieces might touch upon a topic that goes beyond what a particular client needs, but they might know someone else who does.

This tactic works in two ways. First, they will be able to make the connection in their minds between you and their contact with a particular need, and refer them to you.

The other much more powerful way this can work is when your client forwards your content directly to their contact. Someone who doesn't know you may or may not consume one of your content pieces, but they will more likely take a moment and consume it if it's forwarded by someone they already know and trust.

Upgrading Your Service

One simple way to add value to your service is to provide additional insights for your clients as you continue your relationship with them. This content should be oriented towards helping them become better informed, making them aware of features of your service that they may have missed, implementing your solutions more effectively, and keeping them in the know about the latest happenings in your industry.

At our firm, we have particular pieces of content that nobody ever sees, unless they become a client. (I referred to these as Heart and Multiplier in the previous chapter). They speak specifically to questions they might be dealing with while receiving our services, so people outside of this group wouldn't be able to understand it even if they received it.

The advantage around this approach is that just as you sell yourself before the sale through your personal brand and the pieces that establish your authority, the same approach after the sale becomes added perceived value, which they neither had to pay for, nor did it require you to spend additional time or resources.

When one of your clients asks you a question, you should openly celebrate this opportunity. After all, if you get a question from one client, it often means that some of your other clients might be wondering about the same topic. Think about turning that question into a valuable piece of content that you can share with your other clients.

One of the situations in which your client will have the most questions about is when your service involves a fairly long, complex process. Being that your client is not a specialist in your subject, it's likely that they will have doubts about what has transpired, what comes next, and at what stage they're in along the process.

You probably have your workflow broken down in phases, so you can produce a piece of content explaining each specific phase. This helps keep them in the know.

Most people in business don't do anything even close to this! All of the attention is placed on acquiring clients, but existing clients are left in total darkness. This is why this tactic will *really* help separate you from the crowd.

FINAL THOUGHTS

We've just gone through a few reasons why it makes absolute sense to continue selling yourself even after a sale has been closed. If you're consistent with this, you'll have happier clients, you'll spend less effort to connect with new clients, and as a result, your business will grow.

Conclusion

We are living in an amazing time, one in which we are rewarded with more business just for being *more human*. Imagine that!

If I were to be asked for a "secret insight" that has helped me expand and grow, I would say without a shred of doubt that people today want to deal with other people they can like and trust.

The times in which consultative professionals have had to hide behind a corporate logo just to have significance are gone. Corporate logos and entities are just a commodity, which anyone can get with very little effort. What isn't a commodity is the stuff you're made of, that prime matter inside of you that makes you unique, vital, and irreplaceable.

You are allowed to put your true self out there, and by doing so, you will find the solution to most of the business issues you're dealing with right at this moment. Do you need more clients? Do you need help closing more sales? Do you need more stability with your current clients? Do you yearn for more respect within your field? Developing and positioning yourself is the way to answer all of these questions in a manner that actually makes sense and is sustainable in the long run.

Instead of investing your energy into patchwork solutions that will just give you a quick fix, you must continue to develop yourself. After all, *you* are always there wherever you go in your business!

For so many years, I made the mistake of thinking that to have success in business, I had to become someone else. I tried and tried to be that other person whom I perceived to have more success in their career, and I did a really poor job at it. I shut down my true self and tried to act like other people did. It turns out I unconsciously had decades of practice at being myself, so it was much easier to just be myself. Would you believe that?

When you develop your brand, you will not only notice how your professional and business lives becomes much easier, but you'll also find that you begin to "click" with more and more people who will respect you for who you are. There are millions of people right now looking to do business with you; not with what you're selling, with YOU.

If I could recommend one last tip as we arrive at the end of this book, it's to not set this aside as something you'll do some day, when you feel like it. Most people will fall into a rut and pay more attention to tasks they see as directly billable.

I can assure you: Developing your personal brand *will* impact your billing. You need to treat it just like all of your other business and personal projects, because it really is *that* serious and life-changing.

Right now, go to your favorite task management application or to-do list, and add a new project category called "My Brand." As you begin each week and look over everything you need to get done, ask yourself "What can I do this week to develop my personal brand further?" Do this right now, before you forget. Then every time the task comes up, refer back to this book to see which tasks you can work on.

If you haven't done so, don't forget to test yourself in our personal brand report card at http://cstps.co/personalbrandreport. This will be a great starting point to assess where you are and where you need to do the most work.

To close out this book, I just want to say that if I can help you in any way, it would be a true pleasure for me to do so. Just write me an email: alex@ymmymarketing.com, or follow me online here http://cstps.co/followme.

All the best!

About the Author

Alex Rodríguez (@AlxRodz) has dedicated over two decades helping brands and their leaders transform their brand and grow their business further.

Throughout his professional experience, he has created successful experiences for global brands, which have produced millions of dollars in sales in record periods of time.

Alex has created strategic digital content for brands in 4 different continents and 3 separate languages (English, Spanish, and Mandarin).

He has received some of the most distinguished awards in Web, Advertising, and Social Media.

His first book is *Digital BACON*, and shortly after he self-wrote the Spanish edition *BACON Digital*. Between the two languages, these books reached Amazon's bestseller status in four different categories. His second title *Five Fresh Ideas To Dominate Digital Advertising* reached #1 on Amazon in the "Advertising" category upon launch.

Alex is a bilingual speaker, and has spoken at events such as TEDx, The Future of Advertising, and many other important events. He is also frequently booked to hold workshops and mentorships to help develop brands, raise profiles, and launch products and ideas. His methodology is used as training material in North America, the Caribbean, Europe, Asia and Oceania.

He writes about how to strategically attract audiences at CreativeStrategyTips.com .

Alex heads up the team at YMMY (ymmymarketing.com), a creative digital firm based in Florida, USA.

CPSIA information can be obtained
at www.ICGtesting.com
Printed in the USA
FFOW02n0355081117
43408341-42025FF